W9-BAK-136

Before the Dawn

+ Plácido Rodriguez, cmf.
Feb. 2009.

Before the Dawn

~

Autobiographical Reflections
by Eugenio Zolli
Former Chief Rabbi of Rome

IGNATIUS PRESS   SAN FRANCISCO

Cover art: Photograph of Eugenio Zolli by Corbis;
Photograph of Rome © iStockPhoto.com

Cover design by John Herreid

Reprinted in 2008 by Ignatius Press, San Francisco
ISBN 978-1-58617-287-9
Library of Congress Control Number 2008933484
Printed in the United States of America ∞

Contents

Part III: Rome

Foreword

By Roy Schoeman

The waters of Cape Horn at the tip of South America are among the most turbulent and treacherous in the world, for that is where two great bodies of water, the Atlantic and Pacific Oceans, meet in collision. This image provides an apt one to characterize the life of Rabbi Israel (later Eugenio) Zolli, for the story of his life unfolded in a time and place where not only one, but three opposing pairs of powerful conflicting spiritual forces met and collided.

He lived in a place—Rome under the Nazi occupation —where one of the most anti-Christian movements of all time, Hitler's Nazism, came face to face with the Vicar of Christ on earth, at the center of the Church's presence on earth. He lived in a time when the negative view of Judaism that dominated the Christian world for almost 2000 years —the so-called "teaching of contempt"[1]—gave way to the current, far more positive view, of Jews as "elder brothers in the faith" (in the words of both Pope John Paul II and Pope Benedict XVI). And in the Rabbi's very own soul (not irrelevantly the soul of the Chief Rabbi of Rome) Judaism itself met, and was conquered by, the love flowing from the

---

[1] This term was introduced by Jewish historian Jules Isaac in his 1947 *Jesus and Israel* to refer to the teaching that the Jewish people are collectively guilty of deicide, for which they are continually being punished. The very different view represented in Vatican II's *Nostra Aetate* is thought to have been influenced by Isaac's 1960 private audience with Pope John XXIII.

heart of the Jewish Messiah Jesus, leading him into the Catholic Church. The story of his life is hence also the story of these three great cosmic battles, and so provides profound spiritual insight into the unfolding of salvation history.

In the battle with Nazism, Zolli was, with the help of Pope Pius XII, instrumental in saving the bulk of Rome's Jewish community from deportation and death. In the battle of polemics between the Jewish and Christian communities, Zolli's writings even before his conversion presented an overwhelmingly positive view of Christ, to the point that an Archbishop said, about his 1938 book on Jesus *The Nazarene*, that "as a bishop, I could sign my name to this book". And as a university professor teaching the Jewish scriptures, Zolli gave Catholics, including many clerics, a positive view of Judaism both before his conversion, at the University of Padua (1927–1938), and after it, at the Pontifical Biblical Institute.

Finally, and most unspeakably beautifully, Judaism and Christianity met in his very soul, becoming one. The vision that led to his conversion provides a perfect visual image of this. He had the vision as he was celebrating Yom Kippur liturgy, the most solemn in all of Judaism. As the closing prayers were being said, he saw Jesus standing in a bright meadow. Zolli's soul was filled with the greatest interior peace, and he heard Jesus say to him, "You are here for the last time." And so it was—a few weeks later Zolli was baptized and received into the Catholic Church, taking Pope Pius XII's baptismal name, Eugenio, for his own to honor the Pope for all he had done to save the Jews.

Thus the union between Judaism and the Catholic Church was effected in the Rabbi's soul, while an understanding of the intrinsic unity between the two, as the pre- and post-Messianic forms of one and the same religion, permeated his understanding. For when asked why he had given up the synagogue for the church, Zolli replied, "I have not given it up. Christianity is the integration, completion or crown of the Synagogue. For the Synagogue was a promise, and Christianity is the fulfillment of that promise. The Synagogue pointed to Christianity: Christianity presupposes the Synagogue. So you see, one cannot exist without the other. What I converted to was the living Christianity."

So this account of the life of Rabbi Zolli is about much more than just the man. It is about the great battle between the forces of darkness and the Catholic Church that dominated the middle of the twentieth century. It is about the heroism and philo-semitism of that hero of the Jews, Pope Pius XII, despite recent false calumnies to the contrary. It is about the evolution of the Church's attitudes toward Judaism, and of Judaism's attitudes toward the Church. And ultimately it is about the greatest love story of all, the one between the great lover of every human soul, the Jewish Messiah Jesus, and how his love, expressed through the grace of conversion, brings about the ultimate unity between Judaism and the Catholic Church.

Foreword to
the First Edition

With this book, *Before the Dawn*, Professor Eugenio Zolli, former Chief Rabbi in Rome, presents us with an account of the events of his life, and those especially leading up to his baptism. Human factors alone can never sufficiently explain the entire process of a conversion. Another agent, grace, a supernatural gift conferred by God through the merits of Jesus, enters to enlighten the mind, to strengthen the will, and to move one to adore Christ, the God-Man, Founder of the Church, Teacher and Savior.

At our first meeting in Washington, August 20, 1953, Professor Zolli and I engaged in a long conversation. He had come to America that summer to give Biblical Lectures at the University of Notre Dame in Indiana. After a brief exchange of greetings, we recalled memories of persons and events in Rome. Then—I do not remember how—the conversation turned to Saint John, "the disciple whom Jesus loved", and became fixed there. The remarks were in this vein: John was truly the disciple of love, and in Jesus he saw immediately the Son of God as well as the Divine Master. He never abandoned Him; his Gospel and Letters reveal complete and intimate dedication to the Lord. In his Gospel, he treats especially and at length the public life of Jesus in Judea, thus completing the accounts of the other three evangelists. His principal interest is the Divinity of Christ, but he also draws attention to small details that have personal attraction for him and thereby become the same for the reader, as for example, the reference to the time of his first talk with Jesus being "about the tenth hour"—the hour of his vocation—or the reference to the robe of Jesus as a "seamless garment". Finally we spoke of the frequent expressions to which John attaches the same meaning, all concentrated on "charity", the essence of Christian life—expressions such as "to abide in love", "to abide in the light", "to do the truth", "to know God". These phrases exemplify the sublime truth that the knowledge of God may come more from spiritual love than from argumentation. At this point, Dr. Zolli took occasion to avow that in his case he had come to Christianity by way of this charity, and not by way of erudition; certainly he would admit that his culture had been beneficial to him, yet no human principle would have been adequate for accomplishing so much.

It was *Hebraic Truth* that came to absorb his mind, his life, and one may say, his all. He saw it and lived it in privileged surroundings, experiencing contact with everything it has to offer as most noble and attractive. Trained in biblical literature along with his brothers, first under the gentle guidance of his mother—herself of rabbinical stock—then educated in the majesty of the Torah and the magnificence of the Psalms learned by heart as a child, he found himself, while still comparatively a young man, in the position of Assistant Rabbi. Gradually becoming immersed in biblical and talmudic thought as well as oriental culture, and achieving complete mastery of the language whereof every Israelite is justly proud, the language of the patriarchs and the prophets—of angels and of men, Eugenio Zolli matriculated at several institutes and universities of higher learning, thus attaining the scholarship that eventually justified his appointment as Director of the Israelite Italian Rabbinical College. All these in succession formed the links of memories, friendships, and traditions that naturally combined to hold him fast to the Synagogue and Hebraism. But grace, too, was secretly working.

Dr. Zolli devotes ardent pages to describing the mysterious attraction he felt for Jesus Christ from his childhood, and how a true love of Him sprang up in his soul. "God is love, and he who abides in love, abides in God, and God in him", wrote the Evangelist of Divine Love (1 John 4:16). He tells us that the first glimmer of the light of Christ came to him at the sight of a crucifix on the wall of the poor home of a Catholic boyhood friend, Stanislaus by name. In the course of the years, that image of the Crucified often came to mind, and the figure of Christ became more luminous when he studied the New Testament. At this stage, however, never was there any thought in his mind of entering the Catholic Church.

Far from diminishing that compelling orientation toward Christ, the severe trials that Zolli and his dear ones suffered only served to deepen his consciousness of Christ's love. Among these were the death of his mother, who had been such a lovely inspiration to him, the tragic sufferings and deaths of members of his family and innumerable friends, victims of anti-human doctrines, the repeated interruptions and disturbances in his studies as well as in his rabbinical career, the loss of his wife, and so many other sorrows and disappointments. Nonetheless, a profound impression was being made upon him by the words of Jesus, "I am the light", "I am the way, the truth and the life." Constantly, throughout the long period of these misfortunes, he meditated upon them. Then it was that he began to discover the "newness" of the New Testament, nor did his Hebraism ever present an obstacle to his approaching closer and closer to Jesus of Nazareth. He perceived that in the charity of Christ there were neither differences nor discrimination. In Rome he witnessed the splendid example of this in the work of the Head of Christianity, His Holiness Pope Pius XII. In an astonishing and almost indescribable way, everyone was experiencing the material and moral assistance of the Supreme Pontiff during the recent war years. It was an immense charity that heartened priests, missionaries, sisters, and the faithful the world over.

Before the Dawn, rather than being a complete autobiography, limits itself to reflections on certain events of the author's life, as he so aptly states. These reflections are steeped in the atmosphere of a profound biblical knowledge and penetrating spirituality that, one cannot help but feel, are destined yet to yield their richest harvest. The talent and genius of Eugenio Zolli is reaching fulfillment in his conversion to Catholicism. And his conversion may be considered as a step toward the realization of the hopes expressed by the reigning Vicar of Christ a few years ago in his encyclical letter *Divino Afflante Spiritu*, that there "will be brought about the happy and fruitful union between the doctrinal and spiritual sweetness of expression of the ancient authors and the greater erudition and maturer knowledge of the modern, having as its result new progress in the never fully explored and inexhaustible field of the Divine Letters."

— A. G. Cicognani
ARCHBISHOP OF LAODICEA
APOSTOLIC DELEGATE
Washington, D.C.
December 2, 1953

Introduction

On February 17, 1945, Israel Zolli,[1] the Chief Rabbi of Rome, and his wife, were baptized in the Basilica of Saint Mary of the Angels, by Monsignor Luigi Tralia. Zolli was the Chief Rabbi of Trieste for thirty-five years before coming to Rome. His deep learning in the Scriptures and Semitic literature may be seen in the many books he published. Catholic scholars publicly recognized this learning years before his conversion, when they invited him to assist in the work of the Pontifical Biblical Commission, and in the compiling of the Italian Catholic Encyclopedia.

The former Rabbi is now [in 1945] sixty-five, but fairly vigorous. He was born in Poland. His mother was a German Jewess; on her side of the family there were actually 130 years of rabbinical tradition.

It is no surprise to find newspaper comment on Zolli's action insolent, at least by implication. For instance, it was neither necessary, nor good sportsmanship, for certain newspapers to headline the story: "Voices, Rays, Convert Rabbi to Catholicism". Moreover, it was disrespectful and offensive to millions to call the conversion a "religious switch" since it was the outcome of at least twelve years of serious thinking and study by a serious-minded ecclesiastic of the Synagogue.

Only in the Associated Press dispatch by George Bria do

Condensed from "The Chief Rabbi's Conversion", *The Liguorian* (August 1945) and reprinted by permission.

[1] Dr. Zolli took "Eugenio" as his baptismal name.

we find any reference to the "voices and rays" supposed to have affected the Rabbi. Nevertheless, even if Zolli did use such expressions, they did not mean what the casual reader of the news was led to think, namely, that the convert was a dreamer or crackpot; and that this conversion was to be passed off with a pitying shake of the head. If Zolli did use the phrase, he was referring to interior inspirations he had received from the Light of the World. As Chief Rabbi of Rome, this sincere man had offered himself as hostage to the Nazi forces then occupying the city if they would release several hundred of his fellow Jews. Was that the conduct of a dreamer? Wasn't it rather the action of a practical-minded, self-sacrificing pastor?

Jews, and especially the rabbis of the Orthodox group, do not become Christians light-mindedly, nor do they do so without powerful help from God. Experience has proved that a prospective convert from Judaism may nearly always look forward to severe boycotts from his family and friends and all former Jewish associates. If Orthodox, he may expect even father and mother to turn bitterly against him. They will put him out of their home and blot out his name from their will. If the convert is a member of some milder branch of Judaism, such as the conservative or liberal, his penalty for conversion will be bad enough. Israel Zolli and his wife had to face most of those evils. In reply to a suggestion that he had become a Catholic for gain, the courageous Rabbi said, "No selfish motive led me to do this. When my wife and I embraced the Church, we lost everything we had in the world. We shall now have to look for work; and God will help us to find some."

Therefore, when a Jew is willing to take such a cross as this as the price of his conversion, he makes his momentous break with the past only from rocklike conviction that he is doing what God wishes him to do, and only by the power of God. This is clear in Zolli's case, from his defense of his decision.

When the good Rabbi was asked why he had given up the Synagogue for the Church, he gave an answer that showed he had a keen understanding of his present position: "But I have not given it up. Christianity is the integration (completion or crown) of the Synagogue. For, the Synagogue was a promise, and Christianity is the fulfillment of that promise. The Synagogue pointed to Christianity: Christianity presupposes the Synagogue. So you see, one cannot exist without the other. What I converted to was the living Christianity."

"Then you believe that the Messiah (the Christ) has come?" the interviewer asked.

"Yes, positively", replied Zolli. "I have believed it many years. And now I am so firmly convinced of the truth of it that I can face the whole world and defend my faith with the certainty and solidity of the mountains."

"But why didn't you join one of the Protestant denominations, which are also Christian?"

"Because protesting is not attesting. I do not intend to embarrass anyone by asking: 'Why wait 1,500 years to protest?' The Catholic Church was recognized by the whole Christian world as the true Church of God for fifteen consecutive centuries. No man can halt at the end of those 1,500 years and say that the Catholic Church is not the Church of Christ without embarrassing himself seriously. I can accept only that Church which was preached to all creatures by my own forefathers, the Twelve (Apostles) who, like me, issued from the Synagogue.

"I am convinced that after this war, the only means of withstanding the forces of destruction and of undertaking the reconstruction of Europe will be the acceptance of Catholicism, that is to say, the idea of God and of human brotherhood through Christ, and not a brotherhood based on race and supermen, for 'there is neither Jew nor Greek; neither bond nor free; for you are all one in Christ Jesus.'

"I was a Catholic at heart before the war broke out; and I promised God in 1943 that I should become a Christian if I survived the war. No one in the world ever tried to convert me. My conversion was a slow evolution, altogether internal. Years ago, unknown to myself, I gave such an intimately Christian form and character to my writings that an Archbishop in Rome said of my book, *The Nazarene*, 'Everyone is susceptible of errors, but so far as I can see, as a bishop, I could sign my name to this book.' I am beginning to understand that for many years I was a natural Christian. If I had noticed that fact twenty years ago, what has happened now would have happened then."

As was to be expected, the announcement caused a great stir in Jewish religious circles. Overnight, the once venerated, learned Rabbi who had offered his life for his "sheep", became to some an ignoramus, and to all a heretic and traitor. The Synagogue of Rome proclaimed a several days' fast in atonement for Zolli's defection and mourned him as dead, while at the same time they denounced him as a *meshummad* (apostate, one struck by God) and excommunicated him. Here is a sample of the vehemence with which a Jew was cast out of the Synagogue in the days when the Jewish leaders were still able to wield the axe. Whether or not such a document was read out in the Synagogue concerning Zolli has not been made clear, but even if it were not read, we may be sure that its sentiments were burning in the hearts of the Jews of Rome toward one whom they sincerely believed was now a traitor to God and the Jewish people. This condem-

nation was hurled against the philosopher Baruch Spinoza
at Amsterdam in 1656, on account of his heretical views
about God:

> With the judgment of the angels, and the sentence of the
> saints, we anathematize, execrate, curse, and cast out Baruch
> Spinoza, the whole of the Sacred Community assenting . . .
> pronouncing against him the curse written in the Book of
> the Law. Let him be accursed by day and accursed by night;
> accursed as he lies down and accursed as he rises up; accursed
> in his going out and accursed in his coming in. May the Lord
> never more acknowledge him; and may the wrath and dis-
> pleasure of the Lord burn from now on against this man; load
> him with all the curses written in the Book of the Law and
> blot out his name from under the sky. May the Lord cut him
> off forever from the Tribes of Israel.
>
> Hereby, then, all are warned against holding conversation
> with him either by word of mouth or by writing. No one is
> allowed to do him any service; no one may live under the
> same roof with him; no one may come within four cubits'
> length of him; and no one may read any document dictated
> by him or written by his hand.

To the uninformed Christian, this may appear excessively
severe, but the Jews sincerely believed Spinoza deserved it:
they believe that Rabbi Zolli deserves the same. Though to
many it looks like frightful bigotry to condemn a man like
Zolli, we must yet be wary against hastily condemning the
Jews for this. The Catholic Church also excommunicates
heretics with severe penalties.

Rabbi Zolli, like others who became Christians, was condemned by the Jewish elders because in their judgment he
had violated God's Name by believing that the man Jesus
was God. To be fair, we must give to the Jews of Rome
credit for acting honestly in the Rabbi-convert's case.

Moreover, the Jews have long memories. Their souls are still smarting from countless past persecutions; today their poor bodies are suffering again in a most horrible mass murder of millions in Europe.

Christians most certainly should restrain the temptation to scold the Jews for their treatment of Zolli and other converts; and instead should be compassionate and pray for them, as the former Rabbi and his wife are doing.

Inconsistently enough (or consistently, would one say?), non-Orthodox Jews of today have called Baruch Spinoza the greatest Jew of modern times. Such an "about-face" by modern Jews is no reflection on Orthodox Jews of the past or present. "Reformed Jews", perhaps unknown to themselves, have surrendered the revealed faith of their fathers; they can teach almost anything and get by with it. Since many of them are very hazy about the Adonai Echod (the One God) for whom their fathers surrendered their lives, it is no surprise to find them now praising one their forefathers condemned. Einstein, the scientist, committed the same spiritual crime as Spinoza; yet he, too, is praised and respected by Reform Jews. Now the Orthodox have condemned Einstein, too, at least silently. And they would like to condemn him publicly as they did Zolli, but they reasonably hesitate because they feel their people are suffering enough, and perhaps, because Einstein did not profess himself a Christian.

All the difference between the religious beliefs of devout Jews and Catholics hinges on one question: "Is this Jesus whom the whole world worships as God really the Messiah whose coming was foretold by the Jewish prophets of the Old Law?" Any Catholic who stubbornly denies Jesus is the Son of God will be excommunicated from the Church and in danger of eternal punishment in hell, unless he retracts. Conversely, a Jew who professes Jesus *is* the Messiah, will be cast out of the Synagogue as Zolli was. Orthodox Jews of today believe their own ancient doctrines as completely and firmly as Catholics hold to the teachings of the Church.

It is necessary to point out, for the sake of peace, that although Jews repudiate Jews who have become Christians, they teach plainly that non-Jews (Gentiles) who believe in the one God of heaven and earth, and do *His* will, can enter eternal life, even though their understanding of the one God is somewhat spoiled by their notions concerning Jesus and His mission.

Zolli's daughter, not a convert, asserted in defense of her father, "I don't feel that my father's conversion was a betrayal of the Jews. The fact that he could spend forty years teaching Judaism proves the profound connection between the two religions." Zolli himself said sadly, "I continue to maintain unchanged all my love for the people of Israel; and in my sorrow for the lot that has befallen them, I shall never stop loving the Jews. I did not abandon the Jews by becoming a Catholic."

"Once a Jew, always a Jew", is a shibboleth too often quoted by well-meaning Jews as a sort of proof that a Jew cannot in his heart of hearts ever become a Christian. When Israel Zolli was asked whether he still considered himself a Jew, he answered with the same expression, but explained it in its deeply correct significance. "Did Peter, James, John, Matthew, Paul, and hundreds of Hebrews like them cease to be Jews when they followed the Messiah, and became Christians? Emphatically, no."

A Jew who accepts a Messiah today remains just as much a Jew as he would expect to remain if and when he were to accept a Messiah at some distant future coming. In other words, a Jew who accepts Jesus as his Messiah accepts a Jew, and himself remains a Jew. This may sound strange and even heterodox to Catholics who have only a surface knowledge of Jewish prophetic history and Catholic teaching concerning it. A Jewish convert takes as his Messiah the Jew Jesus who traces His ancestry back to King David without a break: Can anyone be more Jewish than that? The convert accepts a Jewish Messiah who proved His mission was from God by doing the hundreds of things the prophet said He would do; chief among them His unquestionable and numerous miracles and His Resurrection from the dead. His miracles are continued and multiplied in His Church even up to the present moment. Has any Messiah ever done the like: *Could* any Jew do anything greater to put the seal of God on his teachings?

When a devout Jew becomes a follower of Jesus, he changes neither his nationality, which is Hebrew, nor his religion, which is Judaism. Well then, what does he do? He merely brings his religion to completion, as Zolli pointed out: he plucks the ripe fruit from the tree that was planted by God. This is why the former Rabbi was able to say that he had not given up the Synagogue for the Church, that the one could not exist without the other. This is also why he repeated correctly, "Once a Jew, always a Jew."

If there is any notion that must be stressed both for Christians and Jews, it is that Jesus did not give to the world a new *religion*, but only a new *covenant or testament* concerning the old religion that He Himself had given to the Jews. God's very nature forbids His giving to the world, at any time, more than one religion or one way of life and worship.

—A. B. Klyber

A. B. Klyber, himself a convert Jew, today is a missionary priest and a founder of Remnant of Israel (New Hope, Kentucky) No one could be more qualified to tell the inner story of the great conversion in Rome that was worldwide news.

Author's Preface

The figure of the crucified Christ over the altar symbolizes the greatest sorrow the world knows. Truth is crucified; the highest Wisdom, the Wisdom of God, is crucified. Charity is crucified; Love is crucified; God is crucified in His Son.

From the Church of Christ the King, a king crucified, can be heard the plaintive chant of the *Via Crucis*. The *Pietà* is veiled; a veil is upon Mary's face. Nothing is seen or heard except Christ crucified.

> O all you who pass by the way . . .
> Divinity and Humanity are crucified . . .

And yet, Christ crucified, humiliated, outraged, and derided is the highest expression of the Resurrection. In Christ, every sorrow becomes pure and holy; to every wanderer, and to all who die in Him, Christ says: "Arise and walk!" And I obey. With a heart filled with sadness, I rise and follow in the footsteps of Christ.

EUGENIO ZOLLI
Rome, Italy

Author's Note

Any apparently extraordinary events narrated in this book are of secondary importance in the story of my conversion. This conversion was motivated by a love of Jesus Christ, a love that grew out of my meditations on the Scriptures. I should like to call my readers' attention to the fact that neither the Apostolic Delegate's foreword nor the Bishop's Imprimatur can be construed as a judgment of these prelates, or of the Church, upon the nature of the events, or any other apparently extraordinary events, which might seem to be contained in this book.

I wish to take this occasion of thanking for their kind assistance the Very Reverend Timothy M. Sparks, O.P., the Reverend John Rubba, O.P., and the Reverend M. Raphael Simon, O.C.S.O., who encouraged me to write this book; also my valued assistant at the university, Sofia Cavalletti, who typed and revised the first draft, offering very useful criticisms.

I

The Suffering Servant of God

1. Childhood Remembrances

I remember the scene as though it were yesterday. If I could paint, I would make it the subject of a tableau—a child of four seated on a stool in an open space, in front of him a chair that serves as a desk. The little student holds in his hands a volume of no less than twelve hundred pages. It is the prayer book, the Bible, of his father; the biblical text is provided with a talmudic commentary. I should say that the little reader is illiterate; he may be able to distinguish some letters of the alphabet, but not all of them. However, at ten o'clock in the morning he is always at work. In what does his work consist? Whatever it is, he persists in it for two or three hours. If we watch him, we shall see: beginning with the first page, the child lifts it with extreme care, looks at it, and turns it; this he does with the second, the third, to the hundredth page. If he finds two pages stuck together, he uses the greatest care in separating them, and turns first one, then the other. He knows that the thread of the story is lost if a page is skipped.

You must wonder why this child pays no attention to God's beautiful world, to the sun that floods the courtyard, the vegetable garden at the back of the house, and the green fields on one side, where materials have been assembled for the construction of a building. Why does he not join Mary and Charles, the charming children of the doctor in the next house? Both are nice children, and Charles owns a magnifying lens, which, when placed in front of the sun, can ignite a match, and once even lit a cigarette.

Do you know, it is a prodigious thing Charles does? He is almost a magician—

And yet, the illiterate little reader is at his post before his chair, with a serene, undisturbed face, scrutinizing the printed pages of which he understands nothing. If we observe the child's face, we shall see that he does not simply glance at the printed page, at the large letters of the biblical text or the fine print of the commentary, but he contemplates them. He is absorbed in his work. You would almost think he is searching for something. Does he seek the truth, or some truth? It may be.

A few years before, the owner of a carpenter's shop nearby asked and received permission to store a pile of lumber in a corner of the courtyard. On the boards are stacked many volumes according to size—large, medium, and small. The little "librarian" with great patience goes from one pile to another, dusting them, one by one, with a small cloth; as he dusts he turns them over, flipping the pages lightly, airing these volumes from his father's closet. This child, apparently so quiet, feels a stirring in his heart. He yearns for something infinite and indefinable.

I was born in 1881 in Brody, which had become a part of Austria after the partition of Poland in 1795. When I was five or six, my family moved to Stanislavia, Austria, a small city that also had formerly been in Polish territory. My earliest memories are associated with this place. I was the youngest in the family; there were three brothers and a sister older than myself. In other words, I had to look up to the rest of the family. Only years afterward did I fully realize the critical situation in which each member of my family found himself during my childhood. Not only my brothers and sisters, but my parents too were being confronted for the first time with the fundamental problems of life.

When I was very small my father owned a large silk factory in Łódź, ex-Polish Russia. He was an upright man, well known and respected in his own country and abroad. For example, once he wrote to one of the firms that supplied him with raw material and made the mistake of assuring the supplier that he would receive prompt payment. The man was outraged: Was there a man in the world, he wanted to know, who questioned my father's honesty? The workers, too, regarded my father with real affection. My mother used to tell me about them. Once they expressed a desire to meet Mother, and Father took her to the factory. She visited every section and received a hearty welcome. When she returned to the door to leave, she found it impossible to do so, for the workers had stretched a silk net across the doorway to prevent her getting out. Three of the workers then presented themselves and said that she was their prisoner; she might not leave until she gave them a present. Everyone laughed heartily. Then the pretty captive gave her keepers some trifling gift and was released.

By the time I was seven years old, all this was only a memory. Relations between Russia and various other countries had become strained, and Russia proceeded to force every foreign-owned industry on Russian soil to cease operations. Every factory had to be shut down, but the owner was not permitted to convert his property into cash. My father wanted to pay his French suppliers, and my mother gave him her jewels for this purpose. Thus our family was plunged into straitened circumstances when my father was a white-bearded man. He was without capital; no avenue was open to him in the sphere of his ordinary activity. He was anxious for employment, but there was so little that he could do—how could it be otherwise?

My mother had always been a good housekeeper, but she was accustomed to having a number of servants and now only one remained, an elderly woman—a Christian— who stayed principally out of devotion to all of us, for we could hardly pay her. Mother had always been very charitable toward the poor, but now even this activity of her former life was denied her: she could help the poor only by asking others to help them. For her, too, how greatly life had changed!

My sister was very cultured; she knew all the poetry of Schiller and Goethe by heart—but of what use were Schiller and Goethe in her present circumstances? In those days it was not possible for a girl of good family to find employment in an office.

My elder brothers had been taught at home by various tutors. They had been well grounded in biblical literature and foreign languages and—of the utmost importance in the education of a boy in those days—they had been taught to write a good hand!

No, not one member of the family had been fitted to withstand the blow that had fallen so suddenly upon us.

But as it happened, being able to write a good hand proved to be a useful accomplishment. My mother was acquainted with a director in the railways, and through him a position was secured in one of the railway offices for one of my brothers whose handwriting was acceptable and who, moreover, knew something about bookkeeping. The other two went, out of necessity, to Germany, the elder to Berlin, where he was able to find employment of some sort, and the other to Westphalia, where he opened a furniture shop.

I was too young to comprehend the tragedy of these persons whom I loved so much. I realized that the atmosphere at home was sad; I saw my brothers leave home one after the other, but how could I have understood? And then, I too had my economic difficulties. I took much pleasure in buying cherries from an old woman who had a little stand near my school—the cherries my mother gave me at home never had the same taste as those I could buy. The trouble was that I could not always scrape up the ten—or even five —cents necessary for my shopping. But I think that in spite of my tender years, I was more capable than my brothers in budgetary affairs. There was a blind beggar who used to take his place on a street corner near our house, asking alms of passers-by with the cry: "Give a few cents to a poor blind man!" When my funds were insufficient for my cherries, I used to wait for the moment when my father went out, with his cigar between his lips. Posting myself near the door, I would stretch out my hand and, imitating the gesture and voice of the blind man, would plead: "Give a few cents to a poor child!" My father could never keep from laughing, and my cherries were assured.

When I was eight years of age, I attended a Hebrew school in Stanislavia. There, on Sunday, Monday, and Tuesday, the teacher expounded to us the Hebrew texts, which first he made us read and translate. This was frequently accomplished under a hurricane of blows. These texts were the Torah (the five sacred books of Moses) with the comments of Rabbi Shelomoh Jishagi, the Psalms in the original text with ritual rubrics, and others. On Wednesday and all day Thursday, with the exception of two hours, and again on Friday until two o'clock in the afternoon, there was a repetition of what we were learning, under the guidance of group leaders.

I was one of the group leaders, having under me four or five boys. This continual reading and translating helped me finally to memorize everything, so that I knew my Hebrew texts by heart. On Saturday, the teacher took me to the house of the Chief Rabbi of the synagogue, who gave me a kind of examination. The old gentleman would give me a text, show me the passage I should read and comment upon. I would glance at it, and with a Napoleonic gesture return the book; then I would recite the passage and comment on it from memory. As a reward, I would receive a sweet red apple.

My mother belonged to a family of learned rabbis; this family could boast of two centuries of intellectualism. My mother wished me to become a rabbi. She used to save every penny she could from the meager budget of the family, and at the beginning of the month, she would give me an envelope with the money for the teacher. For the Feast of Purim—the Feast of Queen Esther—she used to give him an extra gift of money and a package of sweets.

And yet one morning the teacher, without saying why he did so, stripped me to the waist, put a broom in my hand, and ordered me to stand in a corner near the stove for hours. What was his purpose? No doubt, a moral punishment. He wanted to bring upon me the contempt of my companions, but not a boy even smiled; everyone pretended not to notice what was taking place before their eyes. I did not have the courage to ask an explanation of the master. He seems to have been in some way, at least in his methods, a distant precursor of Mussolini: "The Duce is always right!"

I went home sad. Our elderly woman servant received me with a scornful laugh. It was she who, in a casual meeting with the teacher's wife in the marketplace, had accused me of being too spirited and lively. As a matter of fact, I was languid from undernourishment; only on Saturdays had we a little extra, a little better food. I knew that my mother often denied herself even a drop of milk, to give it to us children. The old servant, poorly paid and poorly fed like ourselves, was a good woman; she loved me, and I reciprocated her affection. At Christmas she would give each of us a slice of yellow bread made of flour, sugar, and saffron, with raisins and nuts. Why, then, had she falsely accused me on this occasion? I did not know. I could only console myself by reflecting on a fable of Aesop's: "The lamb prays to the Lord in the time of creation: Lord, do not give me any weapon of defense, because if I have the means to hurt, I shall wish to do so."

In the afternoon of that memorable day, I returned to school. It was toward the end of the week, and I kept repeating to myself, "Justice: follow justice and fear thy God." In the evening at home, my eyes kept gazing at the stars while I repeated to myself: "But does the *teacher* follow *justice* and fear God?"

A serious question was shaping itself in my mind: to become a rabbi one has to study and to know many things. That is true. But what I am learning is simple, as simple as one and two in arithmetic. Is not the Torah rather something that must be *lived*?

My mother was not so learned, but she loved much, especially the poor. My teacher was more learned and believed that he knew a lot. In later years, I had occasions to notice that he did not know much, that his explanations were often wrong. Besides his teaching, he had a business. Between him and myself an abyss was opening.

My father, who was of a rare uprightness, by this time had been obliged to close his silk factory at Łódź, and poverty grew in my home from day to day. In the evening, my mother would pretend she had had her supper, so as to leave the only dish of soup for him. Later I realized that she had gone to bed on these occasions with only a single cup of tea.

When we went to the synagogue, my father would hold me close to him, and while the officiant was saying, "through the merit of him who was strong" would whisper to me: "Here he means the patriarch Abraham." "Through the merit of him who was bound on the altar"; here my father would whisper, "It is the patriarch Isaac" . . . and so on. His teaching was straight and clear.

It was from my father that I learned the great art of praying with tears. During the Nazi persecution, long years afterward, I lived near the center of Rome, in a small room. There in the dark, in hunger and cold, I would pray, weeping: "O Thou keeper of Israel, protect the remnants of Israel: Do not allow this remnant of Israel to perish!" A reward of three hundred thousand lire, a good sum then, had been promised by the Gestapo for my capture, and I was sought on land and sea. Yet I could not pray for myself, but repeated the same prayer with tears, looking up at the stars: "O Thou, Israel's keeper!"

One night about eight o'clock, I was walking home with one of my school companions; the ground was covered with snow and the sky studded with stars. We were walking briskly to warm ourselves on the way home. I said to him: "What was God doing before He created the world? Why did He create it?" He replied, "See here! Stop that! If you begin thinking about such things, you will lose your mind." I followed his advice, and thereafter before going to sleep I no longer thought of God's work of creation, but instead I dwelt on some text from the Bible. But I must confess that after a half century of my life had passed, I returned to the study of the world's creation. This time also I consulted a companion, but one very different from that fellow school-boy—the Holy Spirit Himself, whose voice is heard in the heart of every one of us. An answer was given me that took possession of my mind: God is Love; for pure love, God made the world.

I was eight years old, and it was two o'clock in the afternoon. The streets of the city were covered with snow, shining and hardened with frost; for me it was easier to slide than to walk on the slippery surface. The sky was gray; more snow seemed ready to fall at any moment. Now and then a wisp of freezing wind whistled with a pitiless sound, as if it said: I am death; I freeze all things.

I was walking along the street that led to my home, where I was sure to find my place next to my father at the family table, and where dear ones were waiting for me. There was always a pot of steaming soup made of potatoes and sea-sonings; perhaps there would be some beans, and, I hoped, a baked apple. There I would eat my supper and listen to the weary conversation of my elders—my mother sad and silent, my brothers and sisters discontented. Or it might be that I would have to answer my father's questionings about the texts I had studied at school. "You know, papa, we have repeated"—repetition abounded in the Hebrew schools of those days—"the passage that I like so well, in which it is said: 'If you see the ox of the enemy sink under a burden, you must assist your enemy to lift the animal up.'"

All this was passing through my mind when I saw, far ahead of me, one of the passers-by slip on the ice, fall, and get up again, brushing the snow from his coat with his hands. The important thing, I thought, is to rise up unhurt. Today as I think of it, I say to myself: Fall, yes, if it must be, but fall on my knees with my eyes lifted toward heaven. But on this day, I was only eight years old. I was glad that he was up, that he had shaken off the snow, and that he continued on his way toward home, where in the shelter of his family he would perhaps have a dish of hot soup waiting for him.

Would it be a soup of potatoes and beans? Would he also have a baked apple with the skin roasted by the fire? I speculated about him, but my reveries were arrested when I noticed a peasant who was ahead of me, walking beside a sledge laden with bags full of something. Suddenly he jumped as if he had been bitten by a viper. Simultaneously, it seemed, his horse fell. It lay on the snow with its four legs in the air; the sledge was overturned, the bags burst open, and now grains of corn were flowing out, forming piles like islands of gold on a white lake.

The man angrily threw his whip on the ground; it was useless to him; one does not beat a horse that has fallen. I looked on all sides to see whether there were someone who could help the animal and the peasant. What could a poor man do in such a disaster? The other man whom I had seen fall and rise again must have gone off in another direction. I could not see him, and the street was deserted. Near the place of the accident there was a tree; its snow-covered branches stretched upward toward heaven, as if, it seemed, in mute prayer for one abandoned by all.

Approaching the place, I drew off my gray woolen gloves and put them in the pocket of my coat; then I bent to scoop up the grains of corn. The peasant was pulling the horse by the bridle in an effort to get it on its feet, all the while shouting like one possessed by the devil. After many attempts, he finally succeeded, and the horse stood on its feet, all its limbs shaking. Then the peasant began to gather up his corn, following his own method, and he did far better than I.

In about fifteen minutes, the work of collecting the corn was done. The man took hold of the bridle and gave a strange cry—strange but not ugly. The horse stretched his neck while the man gave a good push, and the sledge glided lightly ahead over the snow. It looked like a ship sailing on a tranquil sea. That ship was slowly moving away without one word from its captain to me. We had met, we had worked, and we had parted in silence. When I put my gloves on again I saw that my hands were the color of the apple I used to receive on Saturday as a reward for my study. But what connection was there between my weary hands, red with cold, and the apple as a reward for learning the Law? Was it a mere association of ideas, or was there something more, and deeper?

As I walked, I thought: At home they are waiting for me; they will receive me with reprimands for my delay; they will accuse me of playing with snowballs, forgetting father, mother, home, and almost God Himself. They will threaten to denounce me to the terrible master . . . but I resolved to say nothing of what had happened. Had I not done what the Torah prescribed? It says: "Thou must help the ox of thy enemy!" How much the more if he is not an enemy! I had cooperated with my "enemy" in succouring his animal, and it was this collaboration that was important in what was done. And so I continued to soliloquize: You will not say anything at all about the fact, and you will listen in silence to their reproaches; no doubt, they will not understand. Like most children, I was obstinate.

Everything happened exactly as I had expected. There were the reproofs, the threats, the blessing of the bread, the hot soup of potatoes, and a golden baked apple, nice and warm, with two lumps of sugar on top of it.

2. The Stain and the Cross

At this same time I was attending an elementary school in addition to a religious school. Now the elementary school did not provide its pupils with ink. Since a small bottle cost only a few cents, there were no inkstands fixed in the desks; each child was expected to bring his own bottle with him.

One day before the bell sounded which warned: the teacher is coming and the lesson is about to begin, one of the many boys whom I knew came up to me and said: "You have a full bottle of ink; I have only a few drops. Will you pour some of your ink into my bottle?"

"Give it to me", I replied, and I started to perform the delicate operation with all the prudence required. Just as the first drops of the precious liquid were trickling from one bottle to the other, the mischievous boy gave my elbow a sudden push to make the ink flow faster. It may have been a trick to get more of my ink, but if so, the effect was not what he intended. An outrush of the black liquid went, not into the boy's bottle, but on my hands, on the floor, and, what is worse, on my trousers, soaking through my clothes even to the skin.

It would be useless to try to express my feelings. As soon as I could, I took the paper my lunch was wrapped in and wiped my hands; my bottle was now half empty. I could do nothing about my clothes. I returned to my place without looking at the boy, who must have taken himself off at the moment of the disaster. For me he was now a nonentity—a zero. The ink soaking my garments was the only token of his existence for me: in my mind he had no being independent of this. I was neither angry nor provoked. I neither despised him nor hated him. I did not denounce him to the teacher. I cannot say that I forgave him; he had, in my regard, not enough being for that.

The lessons went on as usual with the recess periods between them, and finally the desired moment for dismissal came, and I returned home. I was very sad. I made a sign to my mother that something had gone amiss and I needed help—a sign she understood—and I told her the story. My mother knew that I told the truth; I had learned from my father to hate lies. Mother took me aside, washed me with warm water and soap. Then—another suit. She looked into my sad eyes with a sweet long look of love, caressed my forehead, and kissed me. I knew that she understood me fully.

To have a conscience means to be aware of the bonds of human society, and more important still, to be in communion with God. Before God, whom we love and by whom we wish to be loved, we must not appear ugly, especially through our own will. To be physically deformed is a great misfortune, which merits our compassion for the sufferer; rightly suffered, it may be the occasion of grace. But what if we voluntarily render ourselves morally deformed?

Jesus cleansed the lepers, physically deformed, by saying to them: "Your sins are forgiven you!" That great follower of Christ, Saint Francis of Assisi, kissed, washed, cleansed, and converted the lepers who blasphemed, and when their hour had come, sent them to Paradise pure in body and soul.

I, too, am wicked. I lacked, and I still lack, the goodness that made Saint Francis overcome the horror he felt of the bad odor of the lepers. His goodness was so heroic that he could kiss them, serve and care for them.

This is a critical moment in my interior life, in the building up of my soul. I, now a Christian, ardently and openly a Christian (after living for decades as a hidden, potential Christian), am not able to follow in the sweet footprints of my Redeemer, kissing them with tears. This I should, and do, confess.

I do not hate, but neither do I forgive; because my way of annulling the offender supersedes and renders vain both forgiveness and charity. If I effaced in my mind the black stain made by another under my eyes and to my detriment, in the same way as my mother washed the ink from my clothes, without commotion and without any change in my interior life, I should do well. But instead I annul him who made the spot of ink, and in so doing I suppress, although subjectively only, by an interior act, one of God's creatures —and what is more, a sick creature of God.

Jesus cured the lepers, forgave and annulled their sins because He had received from the Father the power to forgive sins. I annul and I do not forgive; I do not bend lovingly over the deficiency of another, although I bend over my own and try to make reparation. Thus I fail, and what is sin if not failure? I sin even though I know the specific duty entailed by the prayer of Jesus: Forgive us as we forgive. If the Lord forgave me like this—as I forgive—I should be truly in a pitiful state.

The adversaries of Jesus advanced upon Him in the synagogue to strike Him blows. Who can compare His sufferings and His wounds with those of Jesus in His Passion? It would be blasphemous! And yet, He said, "Father, forgive them." He not only forgave but asked the Father to forgive.

Who will give me the strength not to annul, but rather to love what I have not known how to love, what I still do not know how to love? The grace of God through Jesus Christ, our Lord.

Big Joel and the widow's son, Stanislaus, were my companions in my second year at school. The class was a large one, composed of about thirty Christians and six Israelites. One, with very black hair, we spoke of as a *caraita*. The *caraita* pronounced Hebrew with a Spanish accent that both pleased and amused me very much. He belonged to a religious Hebrew sect that did not follow the "oral Law", or Talmud, but we Israelite boys did not look upon him as a sectarian. Those were peaceful times. We Hebrew children loved our Christian companions, and they loved us. We knew nothing about race distinctions; we knew that our religions were different, and therefore when the hour came for religious instruction, each went to a separate hall. When the lesson was over, we all met again.

Today, as I write this, I think with grief of the flood of hatred that has swept over Europe. It was such a lovely way of life to ignore racial antipathies, to have no party revenge or religious intolerance.

The problems that occupied and absorbed our attention in those days were our school lessons, oral examinations, and report cards. The entire class formed a front against our common enemy, the class record. Our slogan was one for all and all for one. Our strategy: to copy the lesson from each other, to consult one another's translations surreptitiously, to prompt one another with answers. Often we sent by air skilfully folded notes bearing such urgent messages as: "We shall say that he gave us three chapters instead of five." He—the teacher—would inevitably find his convictions shaken when we shouted that untruth in a chorus, with all our might. The victory was undoubtedly ours. When the season was over, we all felt a bit proud; we were heroes, victors, all of us; therefore no one was envious of another.

This noble unity of purpose reached its highest triumph during the history hour. The teacher was tall and thin, with a very intellectual face, and his manners were refined. The books he had written and published provided the historical sources from which Sienkiewicz worked in preparing the background of his famous novel, *Quo Vadis.* I still do not understand why the government sent him to us little ignorant boys rather than to a university chair. We twelve-year-olds appreciated in that exceptional teacher a quality that had nothing to do with his teaching. For him, personally, it was a handicap, but for us it was a great help in the question period. This learned teacher was almost deaf. He would call upon one or another of us. As the boy stood at his place to answer the question, the teacher would read his lips—or perhaps he would not. Each of the ones questioned would speak very fast, talking all kinds of nonsense, sometimes sending to the devil both the learned historian and the whole of history, ancient, medieval, and modern. It sufficed to speak fast while the poor man nodded his head in assent: a head so full of knowledge and understanding. But he was contented, and so were we.

The unity of the class was evident from the austere aspect it took on. No one would move; it looked like a gathering of living statues, all eager to learn. One Friday morning, the notice on the school bulletin board read, "History class from 10 to 11." The hour of ten came. Near me was a big boy, also an Israelite, named Joel, who was chewing with strong jaws some Sabbatical sweets that his mother had given him for his lunch. A Christian boy was answering the teacher with the usual stupidities. When he had finished, the teacher said: "Well, sit down. It is clear you have studied." And of course, the mark was excellent.

And now Joel was called. Poor boy, with such a prophetic name! He made an unspeakable effort to swallow in one gulp the large piece of candy he had in his mouth. There he stood, a big boy with broad shoulders and large eyes: he was the oldest boy in the class. "Tell me something about Napoleon's expeditions in Russia!" That was a good question: Joel was the very man for such scientific considerations. He began to say foolish things, one after another with lightning speed, his enthusiasm growing as he talked. The teacher approved with frequent inclinations of his head that indicated assent. All at once, like a bolt of lightning from a blue sky, the teacher said:

"Come and point out all this on the map."

The most expert geographer could never find on any map the itinerary my learned friend had described. A big hairy hand began to travel up and down, right and left, over the Russia of the Czar. "I see that you have not opened your atlas!" remarked the teacher. And the mark was a zero. Joel was a wounded lion, and the consternation was general. Whose turn now? At that moment, the saving sound of the bell announced the end of the lesson. All were saved except big Joel.

Stanislaus and his mother lived on the ground floor of a house in the suburbs. Once or twice a week I would go to spend the afternoon with Stanislaus. Sometimes another companion would come also. The modest home had something in it very attractive for me. I was happy there. There was only a large, square room and a small kitchen; that was all. The walls were white; a long table covered with un-bleached linen had a very neat appearance; along the table on either side long benches of natural-color wood took the place of chairs. In a corner stood a wooden chest, painted white. In the middle of one wall hung an inexpensive clock, and a little above it, a crucifix of plain wood, with the branch of an olive tree over it.

Two of us boys, sometimes three, read our Latin texts, did our homework, studied our lessons in history, geography, and algebra. From time to time Stanislaus' mother would come in to exchange a few words with us. I remember that she was always dressed in black. She had become a widow many years before; her husband had been employed on the railroad.

"Now have a rest", she would say; or "Now go back to your studies, and I shall return to my sewing." Then she would retire to the kitchen, after mother and son had exchanged an affectionate glance. Both spoke little. Their relations were marked by a certain reciprocal respect.

How often had I not heard mothers use bad language and strike their children! These two understood each other without words. We often noticed a little sadness, something we perceived by intuition; it was in the atmosphere. Yet they never seemed worried, or preoccupied, or grieved. After the death of the father those two—mother and son—did not seem to ask much of life. The mother provided the necessities with her widow's pension and her work. She had a beautiful face, an olive complexion and large black eyes, expressive of peace. Stanislaus was good, gentle, studious, and intelligent. I felt that he and his mother liked me.

We boys never became boisterous or disorderly during our study or in the intervals. It seemed that in that white room, and in the presence of the crucifix, one could not

help being serene, gentle, and good. Sometimes—I did not
know why—I would raise my eyes to that crucifix and gaze
for a long time at the figure hanging there. This contem-
plation, if I may call it that without exaggeration, was not
done without a stirring of my spirit.

Why was this man crucified? I asked myself. Was he a bad
man? Are all the wicked crucified? Why did so many people
follow him if he was so wicked? And why are my mother's
"ladies" (I shall explain the meaning of this term later on),
who follow this "crucified one", so good? How is it that
Stanislaus and his mother are so good, and they adore this
crucified one? Why do we boys become so different in the
presence of this crucifix? And in the company of Stanislaus
and his mother? How is it that his mother deals with him
without harsh words or blows? My own mother, although an
Israelite, kept in her heart certain mysteries that she shared
with me. Occasionally she would ask me to keep them as
secrets from my father and brothers. It was thoughts like
these that would pass through my mind as I gazed at the
crucifix.

This crucified one, moreover, awakened in me a sense of
great compassion. I had the same strong impression of his
innocence as of his pain . . . he agonized. He made me think
of a neighbor of ours, Mr. Orrone—my father prompting
him with the prayer "Hear O Israel" in a firm voice, one
word at a time; Mr. Orrone repeating the words in a feeble
whisper. He was suffering from sores that had become gan-
grenous, and he knew he had to die. The Lord God "delivered him at last", as my relatives put it, talking among
themselves; he was freed of pain, and that was well.

But this man on the cross did not die of sickness; he was
young. He bows his head, he is very tired, and a sweet sleep
is about to envelop him. He does not cry out in his pain,

he does not lament, he does not curse. On his face is no expression of hatred or resentment. The olive branch above his head seems to whisper softly of peace.

No. He, Jesus, that man—now he was "He" for me, with a capital H—He was not bad; He could not have been in any way wicked. Perhaps He was, or perhaps He was not, the "Servant of God" whose canticles we read at school. Perhaps He was, or perhaps He was not, that sufferer of whom the master told us briefly: "It is King Hezekiah, or the people of Israel." I did not know. But of one thing I was certain: He was good.

But then, why did they crucify Him? In the book of Isaiah there are four canticles—42:1–7; 49:1–5; 50:4–9; 52:13— 53:12—which present to us an innocent man, purer than any other in the world. He is stricken and humiliated, exhausted by so much suffering; he dies in silence as in silence he suffered. Then the crowd seems to recover from its fury: "Why have we tormented and put to death Him who bore our sins?"

To speak and say nothing, to be silent in order not to reveal, is an art not reserved exclusively to diplomats. Many times I have seen my mother say a kind word at the very moment when she could have complained. In a sense, she was isolated in the midst of her family, for whose members she was continually sacrificing herself. Her soul seemed to receive suffering as the dry earth receives the first drops of rain— in perfect silence. O sweet mother mine! you drank your tears of renunciation and sacrifice. You were offering to the Lord your suffering; and you desired that your compassion for other people's pain, your works of charity, should remain veiled before God. You did not consider your goodness and your charity as your own property or possession.

As soon as your acts of charity were done you forgot them. You were always giving away your kind deeds as a thief divests himself of his booty. You wished that the Lord should rejoice in the joy of the poor whom you helped, and not because of your goodness. Oh yes, Mother, I understand you only today; you wanted nothing. Your son had a way of annihilating others, but you helped them; you judged no one, and wished to annihilate only yourself. You, so rich in understanding, welcomed in silence the reproaches, the complaints, the lamentations of others, wishing only to associate the pains of others with your own. You loved charity and hated all evil, all intolerance, all that was ugly. You performed acts of ardent charity; you sacrificed yourself; but the fervent desire of your soul was to detach yourself from your works, if possible, even in God's eyes. Today I see and appreciate the great mystery of your soul; I take hold and steal from you the secret of your life, and in exchange I offer to you my own burning tears. Accept them; they are the sincere tears of the son you loved.

You walked this earth with a light step, scarcely touching it; you were not yet in heaven, and yet no longer of this earth. Like the biblical mourner, you, Mother, have been a stranger in the midst of your brethren. You were with them, for them, in them, and also outside them. Alone with God and with God alone. Today, when I am not far from the border between life and death, I live again fully. You live in the great Light of God alone, and here below you live in my soul.

On this earth, no one of your dear ones is left but me. Of your other sons none died a natural death; only your youngest daughter, whom you yourself prepared for death. All your sons fell victims of the hatred of the Nazis. Now you are waiting for me, sweet mother mine, for me alone.

3. The Sins of the World

It was a Friday in midwinter, at four o'clock, when evening begins to draw in; from the sky, large flakes of snow were falling, passing one another and dancing in circles, meeting and separating. The snowflakes seemed like so many butterflies playing hide-and-seek. The air was still and the cold moderate. I was a small boy, happy to be walking in the midst of that whirling of white butterflies; they seemed also like white rose petals, falling and drifting. Every child is something of a poet, and on this occasion, I was also something of a philosopher. Who knows, I thought, but those snowflakes may be stars coming down for the fun of dancing with me in the air? But why do they rest on the ground? Will they return to the sky in some other form? Senseless fantasies! But there was a reality better than any fantasy to which my thoughts turned: this evening my father would say to me: "Come, let us go!" And my mother would put on my coat, cap, and gloves, and I would go to the synagogue with my father. Out into the snow again, and the flakes would whirl around me, pause on my coat, my cap; and a few, more playful than the others, would light on my nose. I liked that!

But shortly after that momentous "Let us go!" that evening, my mother spoke: "It may be better to have the child remain at home with me. We shall pray together." Then the answer came, "As you say!"

Oh, poor me; and there is nothing I can do about it! My father goes, and I am left with mother at home. So we

pray awhile, and then behold a surprise! Mother goes to
the kitchen; I follow her, of course. She comes back with
a good-sized basket, large enough to hold a tureen of hot
broth, half a chicken, and a piece of boiled meat. Around
the tureen are rolls of white, homemade bread. In a corner
of the basket is a dish of stewed fruit. We set out, my mother
and I; with one hand she holds the basket, and her other
hand clasps mine.

We arrive at our destination; we go down a few steps into
a basement dwelling. There is a table and on it two lighted
candles and some brown bread. "The food must be poor in
this house", I think. I see a knife but no forks or spoons.
"Do they eat here?" I wonder. My mother approaches the
sick woman and kisses her. They talk together for a few moments. Then my mother places the basket near the bed. Soon
other members of the family arrive. "Good Sabbath!" says
the husband of the sick woman. "Good Sabbath", say the
children. Mother answers, "Good Sabbath", and we leave.

Mother has "forgotten" the basket she set down near the
sick woman's bed. What will happen to it among those hungry people? I wonder as we walk along, my hand in hers.
We walk fast now, as we wish to reach home before Father
returns from the synagogue. In the one he goes to, they sing
a great deal, so we hope to be home in time.

We have arrived before Father. I put away my coat and
cap; then I sit near the burning candles with an illustrated
Bible. Mother also takes a book for herself, after having put
her finger on my lips as she has done on the occasion of
previous expeditions of this sort. I answer with my eyes:
I will not breathe a word of it! The pact is sealed with a
kiss on my forehead. After a while, a pleasant "Good Sabbath!" said by my father, which draws a gentle echo from
my mother: "Good Sabbath!"

One particular Day of Atonement had something very special and sorrowful for me. Everyone went to the synagogue.
Could a single Jew be found on that evening who had not,
in company with others, asked pardon for sins? I do not
think so. I alone was destined to stay at home before a table
covered with a white linen cloth; in its center were four
burning candles. In the kitchen, the maid was doing her
work. Why was I alone? A tiresome doctor had said: "He
is better, but keep him home for ten days more." Had he
said six or eight days, I could still have made a contract with
Father and Mother: with the help of a few tears, persuaded
them. But he said "ten", and that was only four days ago.

So I opened the book entitled *Prayers for the Day of Yom
Kippur.* I knew all the important texts and the prayers of
the Holy Day by heart. I found difficult only the liturgical
expressions of the *paetani*—the poets from eighth century
after Christ onward. For these I needed my father's help.
These dear *paetani* do not know that their frequent refer-
ences to passages of the Talmud and Midrash are not for
boys eight years of age. Happily, there are few or none in
the evening prayers of the holy day. I liked the biblical saying: "All the congregation of the children of Israel will be
forgiven, as well as the stranger who dwells in their midst,
because all the people sinned through ignorance." As I was
alone, I could indulge in thinking: The Lord grants pardon
also to the strangers dwelling as citizens with Israel. How
beautiful are the last words: "because all the people sinned
through ignorance". Among our people there are citizens of
foreign origin, and there is myself, a small boy. What pleased
me most was the thought that all sin through *ignorance*. People like to make heroes of themselves; they are like those
big strong boys who bully the littler ones and do all kinds
of mischievous things. But they are greatly mistaken: what

they do is done through *ignorance*. Still, they sin, and sin is a very ugly thing because it displeases God.

I continued to read for a quarter of an hour, and then I came to this: "Place the fear of Thee in all Thy works, and the dread of Thee on all Thou hast created." This perplexed me. I also fear God, but because I love Him—but could I still love Him if I feared Him as I fear the schoolmaster, for instance?

There I am again, talking about the schoolmaster, I thought, even on the evening of Kippur. I ought to be ashamed. I love my father and mother, and in the same way I love God. Dear God, I do love You! So I am not so bad, after all. And is it true, Lord, that You love me? "Our God and the God of our fathers, may our prayer reach Your presence. Do not hide from our supplications, for we, who have sinned, are not arrogant and stiff-necked, saying, 'We are just.' We and our fathers have sinned."

At this point, all my reasoning seemed swept away by love. Those words, "We have sinned", represented for me an indisputable truth. And the weight of sin felt like a mountain on my heart. I shed a tear. Then there followed in my mind, in almost alphabetical order, a list of sins, of many sins. I felt oppressed by them, and I sank like one overburdened. Another tear fell, a third, a fourth, and many more were my tears than the sins I had listed; my tears became a torrent. After a while the atmosphere became lighter, and passing from page to page, I came to the end of the prayers for the Day of Atonement. Then I kissed the book and went to bed.

But I could not sleep. I felt such great sorrow, and I had cried bitterly at the words: "We have stolen". Then I thought: *I* have never robbed anyone. And then the terrible words: "We have used violence . . . We have given evil counsels"! But I do not give counsels to anyone; I am too stupid. Yes, I am; and if I could give counsels, I would certainly give good ones. Why, then, did I feel so keen a sorrow? Whence did those tears come? Happily, it was before the Lord that I wept. I understand it now. There are many who sin, who continually displease God, and they do not know that they must ask pardon of the Lord God. God is good, and so I pray for them—and He will forgive them their sins. Perhaps the good God has already forgiven them because He is so good; then I am truly happy.

So I pulled the covers up to my ears; my eyes were heavy with sleep. I heard my dear ones returning, but I would not put off the sleep that weighted my eyelids; moreover, my mother might ask me, "Why are your eyes so red?" So I kept them closed. My mother did come to me; she looked at me and said in a whisper, "Sleep, my little one." She fixed my covers, and after a few seconds I was truly asleep.

The reason for the tears over my confession of sin was clear enough, at least on that occasion. I had made no distinction between sinners, Hebrew or Christian. I addressed myself to God as the One who forgives the sins of the world: *"Qui tollit peccata mundi"*. For a child of that age, this is singular.

My mother, moved at the sight of other people's misery, multiplied her works of charity, and being unable to provide for them alone, had recourse always to the same four ladies in the neighborhood, of whom two were "born" Catholics and two were Israelite converts to Catholicism. Mother asked their help in providing firewood, bread, butter, and a little money, silver or copper.

Why did I so often think of the crucifix in Stanislaus' home, affirming to myself, with a lively feeling of sympathy, "He was good, He could not have been bad"? More than once I saw again in spirit that thorn-crowned head, the blood-stained face—gentle, exhausted, the eyes half-closed —and I would ask myself: But *why*?

Of Christ I knew only one thing—a simple approach to the problem, but one that lent no clarity (among my Israelite people one does not speak or ask questions)—"Christ is of interest to the Christians, not to us." My mother reminded the woman who served us of the hour of Mass. At Christmas there was an exchange of gifts between the Christian woman and us children. We had the greatest regard for Catholic priests and their religion—"the Christians' religion", we would say.

4. He Calls Me

I was about twelve years old. An invisible Someone had begun to knock on the door of my soul. I felt a great void; spring, the green meadows, the flowers which we gathered for the collection every pupil was obliged to make by order of the teacher of botany, the evening sky with its white stars, the struggle of my father and mother to keep at bay the poverty which was becoming more and more acute and persistent, all these sharpened my sense of void and of abandonment.

One day I was wandering alone in the fields when I began to feel a strange longing like hunger, not for bread, not for the companionship of my young charges (I gave lessons to earn a minute salary, which I brought home to my family); it was not even hunger for the sacred texts. It was a desire for peace and death. My heart seemed closed. My companions were different from me. With them I could talk of school, but of nothing more. Even my mother was set far from me; I did not want to aggravate her suffering by describing to her the agony of soul I was experiencing.

I became conscious of the peculiar odor of the earth when it is dry and thirsting for rain, and spontaneously the words of the Psalmist rose in my mind: "My soul is like parched earth, thirsting for Thee." Perhaps, I pondered, I also experience thirst for God. Then, O Lord, why do You not send down Your shining dew, Your beneficent rain, to allay the thirst of my soul's earth? Every morning I said in my prayer, "Blessed is He who takes pity on the earth." On the earth,

I asked myself, and not on my parents? On the earth, and not on a poor boy? Why take pity only on the earth, and not on this heart of mine gripped by sorrow?

I recalled that in the Talmud, in the tract called "Blessing", we read that if anyone says: "We thank You! All thank You!" he ought to be silenced. Then I wondered why that was. In the same way the Doctors teach us not to say: "Your mercy is stirred for a bird's nest." Is this a sectarian theory? Or is it because we should not demand too much of Divine Mercy?

Just then I came to a ditch; I jumped it and was in another meadow, like a green sky studded with stars. Were there not some flowers called stars? It seemed to me that the teacher had said so. How beautiful the ground is! And down there was the villa of Baron N., shining out in its whiteness. The entrance was on the other side; a path covered with white sand led up to it.

But happily the Baron and Baroness were not expecting me. I would not have exchanged my parents for them, no, not even to possess all the white villas in the world. Even at that time, I believe, my mother was selling or pawning some of our table silver, the last remnants of better days now gone. Perhaps, I thought, we shall have some hot soup and a fresh roll. My poor mother! Poor father!

My soul was wounded. I yearned for a kindred spirit. Then I remembered once more the "Servant of God" of whom the prophet Isaiah speaks. I wanted to read and reread those canticles. I thought, Now that I am older, I shall understand them better. There is Job, but he seems further away from me. His discourses are beautiful, contrasting with the irritating and monotonous speeches of his friends. But more beautiful, because more mysterious, is the silence of the Ser-

vant of God. It is a persevering silence that speaks with sublime accents. It is the silence of the earth wounded by the
farmer's plough. It is a fertile silence; it speaks to the heart
as God does, without the sound of voice. It leaves a void
in the soul; it increases the void in my soul, enlarges the
wounds and deepens them and causes them to bleed. We
must listen to the silence of God and of His Servant.

Does God suffer? This is a terrible question. I do not know
if God suffers, but I do know that His Servant suffered, and
perhaps in him God suffers. Then I began to wonder, Who
is this Servant of God? He says he does not break the bruised
reed, he does not extinguish the smoking flax; therefore he
feels the tears, even of things—of the crushed reed, of the
languishing flame, the flame that sinks, and rises again as if
by a painful effort. Poor smoking wick, its strength failing
and its heart filled with darkness; turning to ashes even as
it struggles to give its last light. Poor smoking flax, the life
is exhausted in it before it dies; it fights desperately, trying
to give light to others—to men. How pitiful! And the pity
of it the Servant of God feels fully. The flame of the dying
flax sinks and rises. It is a struggle between life and death,
between being and not being, between light and darkness.
But the bruised reed lying on the ground no longer gives
any sign of life. The dying flame is spending itself; it dies,
and the dead are poorer than the dying. Who is poorer than
one who is dead? The languishing flame looks somewhat
like one dead but fitfully restored by a fresh impulse of life.
But the wounded reed is a dead reed, dead forever.

The Servant of God feels the anguish of the smoking flax
and the unspeakable tragedy of the yellowed reed lying in
the mud, deprived of all life. But he, the Servant of God,
passes in silence, with his heart open, and he receives them
with love. Both are silent: true sorrow and true love. Who

was this Servant of God? The answer brought to my mind the thought of Stanislaus, his white room and of *Him* hanging on the wall.

The sins committed by men offend God. It seems to me that God is wounded; God suffers in His justice or in His mercy. He suffers because of the man who sins, He suffers with the man who sins, because the man's condition is more pitiful than the smoking flax and the bruised reed that moved the Servant of God to pity.

Why had I gone wandering alone through the meadows? The real reason was, of course, to collect specimens for my "herbarium", a kind of cemetery of pressed flowers with classifications written by me like epitaphs. When I wrote the annotation "Linnes" or the title given in the manual we used, with the number of the page, what I ought to have written was "Here lies a pale and miserable flower, N. N., prematurely culled—(date) by me." But I had to write what was agreeable to my teacher: I did then, and many other times later on, what pleased others.

Only my thoughts were my own; only the sadness of life was mine; only the solitude was and has remained mine, even unto this day. These are always mine. No one is sufficient to satisfy man, and no thing is sufficient. You draw near a person and seem conscious of something that satisfies: something draws you out of the prison of loneliness. But in all persons and in all things one finds nothingness, or self-sufficiency, more or less evident. Yet only in the realization of one's own nothingness does one find all, that impenetrable all, which is both disquieting and sweet at the same time; something that both wounds and heals, something that gives the sensation now of void, now of all plenitude.

I remember witnessing the death-agony of a big black dog at the foot of a tree. He was lying on his back, pressing his upturned paws against his body—his breath was heavy, his eyes half-closed; there was not a whimper of lament. Evidently, he was conscious of his end and was resigned. He had only one purpose left to achieve: to die.

Another day I was passing near the slaughterhouse, and I noticed the animals who were being taken there. They caught the odor of death in the air and cried out in fear; they would go no farther.

A dog's affections are keen, often marked with a kind of nobility that we men sometimes lack: fidelity and courage. But, I said to myself, animals do not feel that void, that thirst for the Infinite, which is in me, which an ordinary man feels, suspended between the green expanse below and the blue expanse above. I seem to hear a distant voice calling me; it comes from the Infinite. I hear myself called by Him who sees me and whom I see not; all my awareness is of Him only; He feels me and I feel Him. I am called by Him who is true; His name is Yahweh, the ineffable name, the Being. He who assuredly is, He is. I am, only inasmuch as He is. If He were not, we should not be. He cannot but be. If the sun were not, its rays would not shine on the earth, and I can now understand why the ancient peoples could worship the sun. The Psalmist does not hesitate to say: "The Lord is my Light."

Animals are born, live, love, suffer, and die; their senses are sharper than ours, but they do not know *Him*.

He, the crucified in Stanislaus' big white room, and *He* whose voice called me, calls everybody. In the solitude and peace of the meadows, it is *He* who speaks. He speaks, He calls—only He.

But, I ask myself, are all men conscious of the void in their soul, and do they free themselves by listening to, or receiving, the call of Him who is at once near and distant? This is a strange definition, and yet—His voice reaches me from afar. I am listening like the beloved in the mystical Song of Songs, and hear Him come from on high, from above me, in the air as on the wings of a gentle wind. To me, as to the beloved, He seems to come from the tops of the mountains. I do not see Him but I feel Him near, always nearer. So I go to meet Him, and yet I do not find Him. Then I wait, and wait still longer, and my waiting becomes prayer: it is invocation. I invoke Him, the One whom I know, and yet do not know.

He comes nearer, and my expectation becomes a prayer more sorrowful, more fervent. It is not I who call Him, but He who calls me; it is my soul that calls Him. Who is He? Someone different from me; that is all, I know no more.

So He comes. I feel it; He passes without my seeing Him! I listen to hear His voice, but there is no sound. He speaks thus, like the love of my mother, like the sadness of my sweet mother. There is not even a whisper. No vision, no sound. Would that I could hear one word, only one syllable, a sigh only, such as escapes from my father or my mother. There is nothing, absolutely nothing.

Then I ask myself: Is it really nothing that I am waiting for? A voice answers from within me.

No, you are waiting for the All, and in it you are also.

I, in Him? continues the curious dialogue.

Yes, you, inasmuch as He is in you.

Then, am I listening, waiting, for Him and myself?

Certainly. Your true self, which you must study to know, is in Him. He gives Himself to you within yourself.

Are there in me two boys, two souls, two selves? Or am I—God forbid—mad?

No, you are in no way mad. Did you not notice in the synagogue the torches near the Holy Ark? As long as they

are unlit, they are cold, without meaning. When before the
hour of prayer, the Shammash, or sacristan, lights them, they
become torch and flame; two things. The torch is not the
flame, nor is the flame the torch. They are united to each
other, but the flame is of the torch. You are the torch, and
He makes you become light. The light that shines is His
light; you will consume yourself for Him; you must live for
Him and in Him. Therefore, you are the flame that shines,
and the flame that shines is of that light which is He.

Am I *He*, then?

No, you are not He and He is not you, but you are in
Him because He is in you.

But what if I were not in Him?

You would be the extinguished torch.

How many selves have I?

In the hours when you are lighted, you are the torch, plus
the flame, and the flame with *your light* is one and the same
thing with Him. As a flame you are He, in the same way
as the sun's rays are one thing with the sun, and yet are not
the sun.

All this seems easy to understand, but in reality it is not.
Can you understand problems in mathematics or physics all
at once? No indeed, you say. Here also it takes time, hours
of solitude. You are He in the same way as the sun's ray is
solar without being the sun.

The sun was now setting, so I rose from where I had been
sitting on the grass and looked around. I gazed for a long
time at the sturdy trunk of the oak I had been leaning against;
I could see the grass crushed; I must have been there a long
time, alone and yet not alone. I set off toward home, and
in my heart a light was burning, white and cold like snow.
The sky was tinged with red, and from the entrance of a

factory, groups of workingmen emerged, and from another entrance some women laborers. The grocery stores were crowded; the sellers were very busy, one could hear their voices from the open doors: "A half pound of . . ." I passed on and did not hear the rest. From one store I could hear, "All together it is fifteen-fifty." I walked along like a person in a dream. I felt as though I were hiding a treasure in my heart, whereas the fact was—strange association of ideas—that to cash my salary check for the lessons I gave in the house of D., I should have to wait until the 27th, six more days. How glad I should be if it were six hours and not days! Poor little mother, my poor father! And I was only a poor boy and nothing more.

5. "Let All Creatures Know That You Have Made Them"

When I was eighteen, I felt that we must somehow break out of the vicious circle in which all the efforts of my family to improve our finances resulted only in increasing poverty. Some years before this we had moved from Stanislavia to Leopoli, Austria, where we were now living. My high school education completed, I had as my objective the University of Florence. There were, however, insurmountable financial obstacles. I therefore decided to take courses in Hebrew religion that would enable me to teach. I taught for two years before beginning my university studies. By the time I was twenty, my continuing courses in religion had led me to the study of the Maccabean period and put me in touch with the Greek world of that age and its religious thought.

Strange, I remarked to myself, whereas the Hebrew language has no word for "goddess", how much of Greek religious thought is concerned with the infatuations of the gods for beautiful goddesses. Not even the Divine Immanence, the Shekhinah, can be compared to any one of the goddesses of the Greek world. The God of Israel is jealous of the other gods and does not want His people to worship any divinity outside Himself. The Greek divinities are broad-minded; they live and let live.

In Israelite tradition, the steps of man are ordained by God. The Lord gives commands to Adam and punishes him for failing to observe them. The Lord continually intervenes in the events of the patriarchs' lives, liberates His people from Egypt by His miraculous intervention, gives His orders to

Moses, and provides sustenance for the people in the desert; He directs the history of Israel and of the other nations; He makes known His will through the prophets and gives His law. The Greek mind, on the other hand, is tyrannized by dark powers of destiny that drive men to all excesses.

In Israel, the prophets do not hesitate to rise against the king if he be impious, to reprove the coward's politics and his lack of trust in God. But the prophets of the Greeks know what is happening, and they do nothing, they say nothing. Are there any prophets in Greece? The philosophers are concerned with the exact knowledge of nature rather than the knowledge of God. Is it not the same with the myths, which personify the forces of nature?

The Greeks aim at improving the laws of the Republic, they sing of the beauties of nature, but who ever thinks of the city of God? The period of the Maccabees seemed to me to represent a clash between two contrasting worlds more than a clash between armies. Greece prepared the way of science and created art; Israel guards and defends the sacred treasures of the One God.

Hellenism did not find the way to my adolescent heart.

In the words of an ancient treatise, the *Sentences of the Fathers:*

> Every day, like a mysterious voice coming from Mount Horeb, declares: "Woe to creatures on account of the dishonoring of the Law." When Israel congregates in the synagogues to say: "May His great name be blessed", the Lord shakes His head and says: "Blessed is the king that is glorified in his own house. Woe is Me, for I have destroyed My house and have burnt My Temple and dispersed My sons among the nations."

Yes, the Lord God suffers for Israel and with Israel. Israel is still in exile, far from the Promised Land.

There came to my mind the Sorrowing Canticle of Israel Niagiara: "Return to the Sanctuary, to the *Sancta Sanctorum*, the place where the spirit and soul are delighted; there they will sing to Thee sweet songs, in Jerusalem, the city of beauty."

The literature of the Midrash has some stirring pages on the Messiah in chains, who, in exile for God, meets Him in the middle of the night. Every step of the Messiah is accompanied by the clanking of the chains that bind Him.

There, also, is to be found the figure of the Leper-Messiah at the gate of Rome: he bandages and rebandages his sores one at a time, wishing to avoid delaying the hour of liberation, which will come suddenly.

At other times the teaching of the ancient doctors sounds desperate: "There is no Messiah for Israel, because He was already 'consumed' in the time of King Hezekiah." Assisted miraculously by the Lord against his enemies, King Hezekiah should have intoned a new canticle, but instead he merely made his own the psalm of David: "Now I know that the Lord helps His Messiah with His saving arm." The king did not proclaim himself Messiah, and so for the failure in initiative of a man in the past, there is no longer a Messiah to come.

How different is the Messianism of the prophets. There the Messianic king breathes the fear of God and judges not by hearsay nor as the eyes see. He strikes the earth with the rod of his tongue, and with the breath of his lips slays the impious, and spreads a sweet peace over all the universe. Peace and tranquility are everywhere, and the earth is filled with the knowledge of the Lord, as the sea is filled with water. How deeply this impressed me! And I yearned for a knowledge of the Lord, a knowledge through love.

He who loves turns to the beloved, wants to be in communion with the beloved, in intimate communion, sharing a common feeling, and so the idea of the sorrow and sadness of God tormented me.

The courses preparing me for my degree as a Master of Religion also took me into the field of Hebrew Religion and Philosophy of the Middle Ages. I thought to myself: this philosophy—for instance, that of Maimonides, the "Great Eagle", in his *Guide for the Perplexed*—is someone else's philosophy; perhaps the Greeks'. It was made use of to strengthen God's truth, and to prevent the Hebrew contemporaries of Maimonides from being lost in the mazes of Greek philosophy.

I knew nothing of Scholastic Christian philosophy; only later did I learn that between the Hebrew and the Christian currents there had been many contacts, and that the Christians philosophized about God.

I understood that I should not demand too much of my colleagues concerning the Great Eagle, but I trembled when I tried to follow their thought. It seemed as if they were going to photograph God with their camera composed of syllogisms. How could one say that God is the "mover immovable"? To me this suggested the idea of a disabled automobile. I thought, My mind must be very weak indeed, since I cannot follow them. I remain behind like a soldier wounded in the battle, entrusted to the Red Cross.

But I *feel* God. Do I love Him? I cannot say. I seek Him with my heart, which I keep awake. There is a force of adhesion that makes the root of the plant cling to the soil, the rain to the earth, the stars to the sky, the drops of dew to the blade of grass, that makes me pick a few flowers and give them to my fair cousin, who plays the piano with such great feeling.

There are in nature (and I realized it at seventeen, before I knew Saint Paul's Epistles and the canticles of Saint Fran-

cis) the accents both of travail and of joy; the joy is shot
through with sorrow, and from the travail sparks of joy like
gold shoot upward. There is at once sorrowing nostalgia and
serene consolation in tears. I know how to weep alone, to
weep over a nostalgia for things past that I have missed, that
never were mine, nor ever will be mine.

And I know how to smile and to thank God for the strange
tears shed for things past that are not mine. And in the song
of joy as well as in the tears, there is a nostalgia for Unity,
for that Unity to which I can give no other name than God.
And men would rationalize my God with the philosophy
of Aristotle? Those were terrible years for me: the thought
of the Great Eagle, so majestic, and I a mere gnat in the air
alone, amid the luminous rays of God's Sun! In my heart
there echoed the liturgical chant in Hebrew: "Let all creatures know that You have made them; let all beings know
that You have formed them."

The synagogue my father frequented was no longer the vast
and spacious one that could hold hundreds of men in the
galleries and as many women. It was called the "Klaus"; in
reality, it was just a school of the Talmud used as a synagogue, in which studies were carried on, a thing not done
in the first, large, more aristocratic, synagogue, which remained closed for many hours of the day. That larger synagogue was poorly heated in the winter. The people were
parsimonious, and they thought it extravagant "to try to
heat the coliseum", as they said.

The Klaus was a large, low-ceilinged room, with long tables covered by unbleached linen, many books, and cande-
labra. People were scattered here and there, studying or in
prayer. The older ones remained near the Zohar or Splendor, the mystical book, with their boxes of snuff. Others

recited psalms and chanted canticles. Another would follow most seriously with a pencil the comments and designs that were meant to assist in the understanding of the measures and quantity of water needed for the ritual bath: *great things*, as they used to say. There was a medium-sized stove, which was always hot in winter. Along the wall was a long bench and a narrow table. Praying here most of the day was a venerable old man, most esteemed by all affiliated with the synagogue. His name was Vecchio, which means "the old one", and his family name was Uccello, which is "bird", so he was called the Old Bird, and not only in amusement. His voice sounded like a whistle.

Everyone knew and helped each other at the Klaus. The young ones were organized as "spies". For example, one Thursday evening they whisper to the administrator of the funds that "Rabbi N. has no money for the Sabbath." And that means, in technical language, "He and his family may have to fast on the Sabbath"; a thing that is not to be tolerated.

Then the bearded administrator opens the drawer of his desk. There are a few bills of small denomination, for which he gropes with fingers stained yellow from tobacco. Through a cloud of smoke, he takes out one, saying to himself: "God must help us!" Then he takes another. Now a young spy goes into action. As if in passing, he casually takes the two bills and returns to his study of the treatise on the "firstborn". Why, I wonder, since he himself is not even engaged to be married?

Rabbi N. is desperate. Do you know what it means to be desperate? You may not be able to guess the cause of his desperation, so I will tell you. He is desperate because, in a most important argument over ritual, he has found two of the "great ones" in flat disagreement. A needle has been found in the large intestine of an animal ritually slaughtered, and the needle's eye is turned outward. There are many opinions available on the subject, a spate of words. There is not a penny to be had for the Sabbath's meals, but this does not enter the mind of Rabbi N.; his whole concern is: Whence did the point of the needle enter, since the eye of the needle is turned outward?

He goes in search of a third "great man" whose learning is in a book in a closet. Now the spy rises, quick as a panther, and while Rabbi N. is engaged in discussion, places the two bills at the momentarily vacant place. The action takes only a second, and the spy is once more immersed in the treatise on the firstborn.

Rabbi N. returns with his book open to the page that throws light on the question of the needle's eye outside the intestine and finds . . . ! He looks around; all is in order. Those who were reciting psalms are still doing so. The administrator (he is a rogue and nothing less) with seraphic calm is adjusting the oil lamps; Rabbi David sighs over the business of that (hypothetical) libel of repudiation which is not clear. Another considers the matter of a firstborn son.

Poor Rabbi N. looks around; prays together with the others. And then? After the prayer, he does not resume his studies. In his heart he acknowledges that it would be better to go home and relieve the worries of his poor wife concerning food for the holy day of Sabbath.

6. The Gospels

In the Gospel I was deeply impressed by the words of Jesus: "I am the light"; "I am the way, the truth, the life."

"Whom do you seek?" asked Jesus at the moment when He was taken prisoner; "I am He!" And they started backward, falling to the ground. Why? Because they understood the deeper meaning of His words: I am the Lord, I am God. Ancient Christianity was right in seeing in Jesus the Name of God, the Name that is the same as God; the Name for whose sake and through whom God created all things. "And the Lord God is the Truth, He is King forever": thus speaks the prophet of the Old Testament. Christ-God is therefore Christ-Truth.

Before His death, Christ sought to learn whether men had understood the mystery of His life. Some said, "He is John the Baptist; he is Elijah or one of the prophets risen again." Peter alone replied, 'Thou art the Christ, the Son of the living God."

Later on, His enemies said, mocking Him, "If thou be the Son of God, come down from the Cross." But exactly because Jesus has a clear consciousness of being the Son of God, He goes *to* the Cross.

The unclean spirits cried out: "Thou art the Son of God." The angel at the Annunciation said, "He shall be great and shall be called the Son of the Most High!" It is a strange thing; angel and demons agree.

The idea that an outstanding man may proclaim himself God is not totally foreign to rabbinical exegesis.

What the Lord intends to do in a distant future, He causes to be foreshadowed by the actions of just men in this world. Sometimes the Lord prevents the rain from falling; the prophet Elijah did this before Him. The Lord multiplies food in blessing it; so also did Elijah. The Lord calls the dead back to life, and so did Elisha. The Lord made a barren woman to bear a child; so did Elisha. The same Elisha, in blessing scanty food, multiplied it.

The doctors of the Midrash Rabbah comment on the question: "Who is like unto God?" (Deut 33:26, 29), as follows: "Israel is, in the persons of the just ones."

But there is a still more surprising rabbinical commentary treating of the dying prophet Jacob (Midr. 2, Gen 49:2). The patriarch called together his sons—through the Holy Spirit. In the opening sentence he says, "Listen, to (*ĕl*) Israel, your father." One of the doctors, changing the short vowel *e* into a long *e*, causes the dying patriarch to say: "God is your father", with the meaning: "*Your Father Israel is God*; as God creates worlds, so your father creates worlds; as God subdivides worlds, so does your father also."

It is certainly an uncommon exegetic audacity, and the commentators try to attenuate it, attributing it to some liberty of style, but this only makes the situation worse. Did some outstanding doctors, whose opinions agree, assert that the patriarch, at the moment of his death, proclaimed himself God? We must honestly answer: *Yes*.

In the same rabbinical commentary concerning Genesis 33:20: "Jacob raised an altar there; he invoked upon it the most mighty God (*el*), God of Israel", this explanation is given: Jacob said, "*Thou* art God in the (world) above and *I am God* in the (world) below."

Quite different is the thought of Isaiah (40:12 and 40:17) when he asks, "Who hath measured the waters in the hollow of his hand and weighed the heavens with his palm?" "All nations are before Him as if they had no being at all, and are counted to Him as nothing, and vanity. To whom then have you likened God? Or what image will you make for Him?" How could the Hebrew doctors think that the patriarch had proclaimed himself God upon earth?

I compared the discourses of Jesus with the rabbinical passages concerning the dying patriarch, and I was amazed, much amazed. In this semi-darkness and confusion of ideas, there was outlined before my youthful mind the problem of the divinity of Jesus Christ.

Jacob did not call himself God, and yet—I saw again in my mind a large white room, a long table covered with a linen cloth; I heard again the ticking of the big clock in the house of my classmate Stanislaus, and I saw once more the crucifix.

I was truly chained to a burdensome program of work, as teacher and student at the same time. Logarithms had become my ferocious enemies, almost personal enemies. And yet I had to struggle with them because entrance to the university was obtained through a classical diploma, and entrance to the university was to be the next step in my effort to achieve economic freedom for my family. I had to give lessons in order to pay for private instruction from special teachers, and I had to help at home.

On the rare occasions when I had two or three free hours at my disposal, I would take my small copy of the Gospels with me and go outside the city. In the midst of the green, all alone, I read the Gospels, experiencing infinite pleasure.

I was deeply impressed by the words: "Blessed are the clean of heart, for they shall see God." It is true that in the fourteenth psalm there is the question: "Who shall ascend to the mount of the Lord?'' and the answer follows: "He whose hands are clean and whose heart is pure." These concepts are similar, but *similarity* is not *identity*. Who besides Jesus had ever said, "Blessed are the clean of heart, for they shall see God"?

The justice of the Old Testament is reciprocal between man and man; consequently, the justice of God toward man must also be reciprocal. We offer and do good for the good received; we do evil for the evil suffered. Not to repay evil with evil is, in a way, to fail in justice. On this point, the life and acts of David are very instructive. In the seventh psalm, David defends his own justice in a prayer to God: "Have I done evil to him who hath done good to me, or have I let him go free who hath been my enemy without a cause?"

What a surprise I found, as I wandered in the green meadow: "But I say to you: Love your enemies; pray for them . . .".

In the Psalter it is asked of God that a rain of fire and brimstone should fall on His enemies like that which fell upon Sodom, and that a strong wind should come to fan the destroying flames. King David wished his enemies to be as the mud of the street. Now I see a man before me, His eyes turned heavenward (the characteristic attitude of Jesus), imploring God to give His enemies good things. From the Cross, He exclaimed, "Father, forgive them, they know not what they do!" All this in an attitude of loving submission: "Let this chalice [which means this destiny] pass from Me; yet not My will, but Thine be done!"

All this was astounding to me. The New Testament is indeed a testament that is *new*.

It appeared to me to be of extraordinary importance, and my mind was intensely occupied with it, even more than with the question of Christ's divinity or the rabbinical exegesis that attributed ideas of self-deification to the dying patriarch Jacob. Such teachings as are inferred from "Blessed are the clean of heart" and the prayer on the Cross mark a line of demarcation between the world of ancient ideas and a new moral cosmos.

Yes, indeed, a new world begins here; a new earth and a new heaven. Kingdoms fall, but the sublime outlines of a kingdom of heaven appear; herein, the rich attached to the earth are poor, and the poor who have known how to detach themselves from the earth are truly rich because they are children and heirs of the kingdom that belongs to the afflicted, to the silent, to the persecuted who have not persecuted, but who have loved.

And I saw my mother as if wrapped in pure flames of love and of silent pain, burning with fever on her little white bed. She was suffering from pneumonia, and the medicine of those days knew not how to fight it. Her large eyes were bright with fever; she asked me if her last hour was near, and entrusted some secrets to my eldest brother. All her thoughts were for my father, now old and lonely. She did not say anything to him that might be the cause of worry, but her eyes followed him tenderly. One day when he went out of the room for a moment, she quoted a verse of a psalm: "Do not reject me in my old age; when my strength is failing, do not abandon me." She was praying for him in this way.

She went out like a pure flame on a pure altar, and of pure love. I felt a hope stronger than sorrow; a religious reverence entered my soul. I thought to myself: *Precious and radiant in the eyes of God are the souls that love Him.* Moved by an irresistible sentiment, I lighted my candles. I wanted to offer to my little mother a homage of light, a crown of flames. Then I drew near to her bed and kissed her forehead, still warm, and in my sorrowing heart there sang the refrain of a great wisdom: *"Blessed are the clean of heart, for they shall see God!"*

II

Florence and Trieste

7. At the Rabbinical College and in the Rabbinate

A few months after my mother's death, before I had reached the age of twenty-three, having completed the entrance requirements for university study, I registered at the University of Vienna. After a semester there, I went to Florence and enrolled at the university of that city in the Institute of Higher Studies, and also at the Italian Rabbinical College directed by S. H. Margulies. At the university, I studied Italian literature under Professor Guido Mazzoni; the history of philosophy under Professor Felice de Tocco; philosophy and psychology under Professor Francesco de Sarlo; Arabic under Fausto Lasinio, friend of the famous Steinschneider. For Greek literature I had Girolamo Vitelli, friend of Williamowitz; H. P. Chajes talked to me about the papyri of Assuan in the Sachen edition (I was the only one who attended this class).

At the Rabbinical College, Margulies was conducting a close study of the problem of "the needle stuck in the colon" or in any other part of the intestine. At other times, he insisted on having us apply our minds to the question of pulmonary adhesions—without ever showing us a lung in nature, in model, or in blackboard diagram.

He read to us chosen passages from the arid stretches of the *Guide to the Perplexed* of Maimonides and conducted unending discussions concerning the making of decisions about young geese—while Chajes waxed fervent on the well-known question of the hen and its affective relations with the rooster, all in view of the egg that was hatched on a feastday. Science is science; it is knowledge, and as such it is valuable, but there are topics of limited interest, at times most limited. How I wished that the hearts of these brave studious men might thaw in expounding to us the "heart's duties" of Baḥya, in giving us a relish for the poem of Guida Levita: "I lent my ear and I believed; I will not question or ask for proofs." Would that they had made me understand the yearnings of man's heart, the thirst for God, and the soul's struggle to reach Him.

In the city of flowers, Florence, I lived gray and cold years in the midst of privations of both body and spirit. Here I received degrees in Philosophy at the university (Ph.D., with psychology as a specialty) and at the Rabbinical College, institutions a short distance from each other.

My writings appeared in the Berlin periodical *East and West*, in the *Marzocco*, in *Israelitic Week*, in the *Israelite Review* —*this* last publication had a scientific tone. All this work was done in Florence. Afterward, I was nominated Vice Rabbi at Trieste.

Around this time, at the age of thirty-two, I married Adele Litwak, a native of Leopoli, Austria, and my elder daughter, Dora, was born to us.

Soon after my appointment in Trieste, H. P. Chajes joined me as Chief Rabbi. One of us was necessary, but two were too many; therefore—in view of the fact that we both were ambitious—the relationship was cool, often tense, and never friendly. He leaned toward the Austrian government and expected to be nominated Chief Rabbi in Vienna in 1918, whereas I was clinging with all my heart to Italy.

When the war of 1914–1918 ended, Trieste became Italian territory. The representatives of the Italian Government and the local authorities heaped kindnesses upon me. I was unanimously made Chief Rabbi; but many were dissatisfied with my appointment, for I know how to love better than how to make myself loved.

No one with a serene mind, free from any pressure of inordinate love—or, still more, of hatred—who examines the soul of Israel as it is reflected in the customs and the literature of her people, can be an enemy to Israel. The important thing to understand is that undying flame of Hebrew nationalism that gives warmth and color to Hebrew universalism. "God loves the people of Israel; He loves the land of Israel", hence, how shall one venture to love the one without the other? In Israelite thought, the Law, the land of Israel, and the world to come are on the same plane. Moreover, he who shares in the possession of the land of Israel is considered as possessing the life to come. The Law and the wisdom of Israel have a superior value if they are taught in the land of Israel, which is considered a source of living waters. Foreign countries do not, in the same sense, possess the Divine Presence—the Shekhinah (Num 9:15, 16); the opinion of a simple shepherd in Palestine is of more value, from certain viewpoints, than that of learned men of other lands, no matter how great their virtue.

And the Hebrew language? It is the sacred language. In it, the word of Creation went forth and the process of Creation is described; the Law was written in it; it is the language of the ministering angels. Some say that by the term "Holy Spirit" is meant the "sacred language".

One cannot read the following passage without a feeling of sympathy and respect: "One of the doctors kissed the stones of the city of Acco; another was repairing its streets for love; another rolled himself in the dust of the land of Israel. At the sight of the devastated Temple, the doctors burst into great weeping." It is no ordinary "nationalism" as the world understands it that is expressed here, no, but an unspeakable sorrow caused by an unspeakable injustice. Israel should not have been disinherited and its people deported and exiled.

Out of nostalgia for the fatherland, it is written that so rich and fertile was "the land" that a certain man walked from morning until night, from one city to another, and —lo and behold!—wherever he went, his feet trod in the honey of dates!

The destiny of Jerusalem is to be the metropolis of nations; the light of nations, just as we think of Rome as "head of the world", the *caput mundi.*

When an Israelite is far from his country, he is, as it were, far from God. The Lord forgives the sin of one who is buried in the land of Israel, and those buried outside the fatherland of old will not participate in the resurrection of the dead. Therefore, to be buried in "Eres Israel" (the land of Israel) is like being buried under the altar. The inhabitants of Eres Israel are free from sin, in life as well as in death.

Through all the vicissitudes of history, Israel has retained her deep sense of election. The soul of the Israelite is always wounded, always bleeding, and therefore sensitive to the point of irascibility—a mere shadow can disturb the peace of a group of Israelites.

All this makes for the exaggeration of the various tendencies within the Israelite Community; it is hard for the rabbi to be *enough* of a Zionist to please the extreme nationalists, *orthodox enough* to satisfy the most orthodox.

8. The Gem Circled by a Crown

The years 1914 to 1918 cover a period of war in the world's history. They also represent a period of great suffering in my soul. I had become the *bête noire* of the Austrian police and of the rulers of the Community who favored Austria. It looked as though I had become a super-Garibaldi, fallen into the hands of his adversaries and enemies. In reality, it was a small thing, a question of political honesty. I had shown my love for Italy freely and had never denied my country; with God's help, I never shall.

At the age of fourteen in Austria, I had been the president of the ABJ, Agudath Bahure Jisrael, an association for Israelite youth, students in high schools. Even at that time two ideas occupied my mind. The first was that the Austrian Empire could not endure much longer, for the simple reason that it wanted to be what it was not, a *national* state, as though there were an Austrian language and culture. Austria should have been like Switzerland, an *international* aggregation. The second thought was that the Jews would not find peace except in a center of their own. I liked the idea of the great thinker Ahad-Haʿam, an idea much in vogue; he wished to see a spiritual Hebrew center in Palestine and a flourishing Hebrew colony elsewhere.

The vigilant Austrian police knew and took note of everything, but I was unaware of it. While I was dreaming, the police were watching. Later on, when Trieste became an Italian colony, the first Italian Governor, General Petitti di

Roreto, received me with particular kindness and friend-liness in an audience. I had the impression that, though he had been in Trieste only two or three days, he knew something I did not. "If I may be of use to you in any way", he said.

"Your Excellency", I replied, "may I ask a favor? We wish to hold a ceremony in the temple to thank the Lord for the grace He gave us in making Trieste an Italian colony. Will you come?"

"I will come with my officers", he said.

"For anything else, at any moment, call by telephone. May I present my adjutant, Marquis Patrizi?"

I learned later how the Governor had come to hear of my wholly insignificant self. The Austrian State Police, caught unprepared by the events, fled to Vienna, leaving behind the secret archives, which were later brought to the Italian Governor. There were also a number of papers filed alphabetically, which contained the "life and works" of several persons. The messenger was charged with placing the package on the Governor's table, and as he could not read or write, he made the last package the first one, and the first the last. My name began with a Z, so that my dossier was the first His Excellency read.

Seventy is a grand number. Seventy is the number of years in a life of normal duration. Seventy was the number of the ancients of the people in the days of Moses. Seventy were the years of the Babylonian exile. According to tradition, the authors of the Greek version of the Old Testament were seventy. Seventy were the young pioneers, the Halusim, the Zionists, who came to Trieste—without documents, without visas, of course—in order to go on to Palestine.

The Community Treasury was empty. No one could leave the Trieste zone without a special permit from the military authorities. The *carabinieri* were beginning to be uneasy, seeing these strange "tourists without visas", with whom no one could exchange a single word. One day at 2:00 A.M., the last three arrived. The *carabinieri* on duty tried to make them pass the remainder of the night in the barracks, but the three did not favor this idea. "We—hotel", they said. I was chosen as the arbiter of their case. "They are good boys", I told the policeman who presented himself at my bedside. "Have them taken to the hotel, and tomorrow I shall take care of them."

I was able to obtain a permit and railroad tickets, gratis, for the guests and for myself. I promised to speak for them to the Head Rabbi, Dr. Sacerdoti, in Rome, and to obtain lodgings and food for them. So I said to them, "Eat a lot. The more you eat, the sooner you will start out." (In Rome as in Trieste, as everywhere else after the war, appetites were greater than the food supply.) The Ambassador, after a few groans of complaint in English, gave the desired visas, and soon my seventy men were on their way, rocked by the waves of the sea.

In the most difficult periods of my life, scholarship rendered me a great service; certainly much greater than those I rendered to scholarship. The temple, the office and the agenda of the office, assemblies, conferences, letter-writing, and lessons occupied my morning hours. In the afternoons, when more correspondence was done, there was sometimes a margin of time for scientific research. During the war, I published a few articles in a good review in Vienna, *Neue Freie Jüdische Lehrerstimme*, which also printed the writings of such men as Güdemann, Samuel Krauss, Optowitzer, Arthur Zacharias Schwarz, all of whom I remember well.

My hours of relaxation and comfort were those I spent in reading the Scriptures, the Old and the New Testaments. The figures that most attracted me were Isaiah, Job, Jesus, Paul. The Psalms were my great favorites. I began to read with relish the mystical book Zohar, which I still enjoy. The text that is used is full of errors, and only Scholem of the University of Jerusalem, the right man in the right place, could provide a good edition.

By this time the entire Bible had become for me like a gem circled by a crown with a series of notions concerning ancient Palestine in particular and the ancient Semitic East in general. In the light of these modest notions of mine, which were continually gaining power over my mind, the Old and the New Testaments were blending into a harmonious whole. The lines of communication between the two were open, and life circulated from one to the other. There were no barriers, nor any frontiers. Sometimes I would say to myself: It is a good thing to be able to see that it is only for the sake of study that epochs and ideas are divided and attributed to fixed dates. The net of lines marked on the maps of the globe are not, fortunately, stamped on the oceans and mountain chains. They are only on paper. How can ideas and words that are immortal be cut in pieces, and how can it be said: This is mine, the rest is another's?

All is of God, and we also are of God. We are from Him and in Him, and He is in us. *Every* greatness, *every* splendor and *every* element of spiritual majesty is of God. God speaks to us through the whole creation, and by means of religious literature, which is itself a kind of cosmos.

I must confess here that I was so far from the thought

of conversion to another religion that it never occurred to me to wonder: Will this literature speak too strongly to my heart? I only know that every evening I opened the Bible at random, looking for a text either from the Old Testament or the New for my meditation. I took whatever I happened to find, no matter where it was. It is in this way that the Person of Jesus and His teachings became most dear to me, without ever giving me the taste of forbidden fruit.

From a simple association of ideas in matters of conversion, without any foolish desire of making comparisons between two persons of different spiritual levels, one great, the other insignificant, I quote from the letter Mrs. Henri Bergson gave the public in 1941: "My husband, who for some time was attentively considering religious thought, and especially after the publication of *The Two Sources* (1932) considered Catholicism with a growing sympathy, had not wished to become a convert for a number of reasons."

Here is what Bergson wrote himself, February 7, 1937, in his own testimony:

> My thinking has always brought me nearer to Catholicism, in which I saw the perfect complement of Judaism. I would have embraced it if I had not witnessed the frightful wave of anti-Semitism which for some years deluged the world. I preferred to remain with those who would be persecuted tomorrow. Nevertheless, I hope that a Catholic priest, if the Cardinal of Paris will allow it, may come to recite the prayers at my funeral. In case this permission is not granted, a Rabbi would have to be called, but without hiding from him, or anyone else, my moral adhesion to Catholicism.

If I have understood this correctly, Bergson sees in Catholicism a step forward beyond Hebraism. Hebraism and

Catholicism are not in opposition but are complements of each other. Bergson preferred the prayers of the Catholic priest, but he would have accepted those of a rabbi. Except for the anti-Semitic movement, he would have become a Catholic. His desire for a formal conversion is evident. In 1917, I was navigating in similar, yet different, waters.

It may have been the beginning of 1918, but I think it was toward the end of 1917—I do not recall exactly. Over my head clouds had gathered: persecutions in the form of "measures" on the part of the Community Administrators, and misfortunes in my family, foremost among which was the death of my first wife, Adele. After her death, I remained a widower for three years. I was trying to drown all my anxieties in an intense scientific labor, and with some success.

One afternoon I was alone in the house, writing one of my regular articles for the *Lehrerstimme*. I was feeling wholly detached from myself, absorbed in my work. Suddenly, without knowing why I did so, I put my pen down on the table and, as if in a trance, began to invoke the name of Jesus. I found no peace until I saw Him, as if in a large picture without a frame, in the dark corner of the room. I gazed on Him for a long time without feeling any excitement, rather in a perfect serenity of spirit. Neither then, nor now after thirty years, could I say what happened in my soul to produce such a phenomenon. I do not seek to penetrate the mystery. What did it all mean? To me now, as then, the nearness of Jesus is sufficient. Was this experience objectively real or only subjective? I do not know; nor am I competent to analyze it in the hope of giving a precise answer. It was like other experiences, under different forms, that I have had since—in 1937–1938, and again in 1945. No doubt such an experience represents a kind of saturation point reached in a continuous interior process of long duration, a process of which I had been unaware.

I had no desire to speak of it to anyone, neither did I think of it as a conversion. What had happened concerned me, and only me. My intense love for Jesus and the experiences I had concerned no one else; nor did they seem to me at the time to involve a change of religion. Jesus had entered into my interior life as a guest, invoked and welcomed.

No denial or acceptance of a formal character entered into my mind. The Israelite Community and the Church represented religious life for me, each in itself. I felt myself to be a Hebrew because I was naturally Hebrew, and I loved Jesus Christ. Neither Hebraism nor Christianity seemed to interfere in my love for Jesus. Jesus was present in me, and I in Jesus.

I do not intend to justify my attitude of those days. It was probably a mistaken one, both from the Hebrew and from the Christian point of view. Neither did Bergson's choice find full approval in either camp. If I too had been facing that problem of anti-Semitism, I do not think I should have been converted, either in 1918 or, least of all, in the period of Nazi persecution.

Conversion consists in responding to a call from God. A man is not converted at the time he chooses, but in the hour when he receives God's call. When the call is heard, he who receives it has only one thing to do: *obey.*

Only in passing do I refer to Bergson, whose conversion, or tendency to conversion, has to be studied in the light of his philosophical thought. I have not the preparation or the competency to do this—I, who am occupied in teaching

Hebrew and Semitic languages at the University of Rome. And even if I were competent, I could not develop such a subject within the scope of this book. Of Bergson I cannot say whether (to borrow the apt expression of M. E. Boisnard, O.P., in regard to Greek philosophers) "the step that takes him to God is a movement purely intellectual." But I can and should say this of myself: I, being a man fed on biblical and talmudic thought, and on oriental culture, found that a deep, spontaneous love for Jesus had entered my heart. "I to my Friend, and my Friend to me." Nothing premeditated, nothing prepared: There was only the Lover, Love, the Beloved. It was a movement arising from love, an experience lived in the temperate light of love; all was accomplished in the knowledge that love gives.

9. Conversion a Renewal

The period of 1918 to 1938 was one of great labor in my office, often undermined by intrigues; and it was also a time of intense study and research. First I was appointed an authorized university tutor; later I was made Associate Professor of Hebrew Language and Literature, and after that, of Comparative Hebrew and Semitic Languages, at the University of Padua. A large number of my students, among them many priests, remain my friends today. Even at that time, they were remembering me in their holy Masses, asking God (as they told me years later) for my conversion.

It was also at this time, in 1920 in fact, that I married again, three years after the death of my first wife, Adele. My present wife, Emma Majonica, was born in Gorizia, northeast Italy, the daughter of Professor Enrico Majonica, archaeologist, friend of Mommsen, Nissen, and Lanckoronsky.

I published some preliminary studies in various Italian and foreign reviews, accounts of oriental congresses and of scientific associations, and these writings resulted in two of my books, among others: *Israel: A Historical and Religious Study* (1935) and *The Nazarene*,[1] an exegetical study of the New Testament in the light of Aramaic and rabbinical thought (1938).

The book *Israel* contains some chapters describing stages in the development of my thought; they serve today to reveal to me the extent to which I then acted unconsciously,

---

[1] An English translation was published by the B. Herder Book Company, St. Louis, Mo.

and how conscious I am of my mental processes today. Concerning monotheism I wrote: "Israel's monotheism does not spring from a reasoning mind, but from a heart on fire." And elsewhere: "A monotheistic conscience such as that of Israel, a conscience that becomes fire—fire that illumines, burns, consumes, draws—cannot be the result of reflection."

During the years 1930 to 1938, when I wrote the foregoing lines, my interior life became very intense, and I was aware of something new drawing me, something that was lived by me and that I could not explain. I wrote then what I should like to say today to those who, not understanding me, have felt it their duty to speak against me: "The religious fact that lives in the depths of the individual conscience cannot be put into words. It is indescribable, because it is not the fruit of cold reasoning or of patient research, or of experiments logically ordained to the purpose of acquiring knowledge." Thus it is not possible to pierce the mystery of the religious living, the religious conscience of another, with the sword of logic. The revolutions in the spiritual life, whether of an individual or of a social body, take place through a process as natural as the entering of a rift of light into a bank of clouds. Usually one does not live a spiritual life of schematic integrity, in accordance with deliberate logical processes. Who can consciously determine the manner in which he breathes, or be aware of the blood circulating in his veins; who can make plans and calculations in regard to such things? How shall one command the light, the rising and setting of the sun, the sprouting of a grain of wheat under the ground? A religious reality such as Hebrew monotheism springs from a spontaneous yearning after truth, and of it is born a special religious history, rich in ideas, concepts, and events. In this the yearning of entire generations is expressed; there are long periods of nostalgia, a thirst for God, a passionate stretching toward an eternal mystery, which later will be summed up in one Person— the God-Man. Chosen souls, distant in time and space, are united by an indivisible but indissoluble thread, that of a common ideal.

The soul of Israel is not drawn toward minute inquiry, toward the critical and analytical examinations proper to the scientist and the philosopher, but it stretches forth with desperate urgency toward the comprehension of the whole, toward the penetration of the great mystery of life in all its tremendous, lofty, and terrible majesty.

God calls man, He seeks him for a long time, and man answers: "Here I am!"

It is man who is poor, in need of God's great light, who comes to God's door. The beggar at God's door stops and gently knocks, to receive the bread of God and slake his hunger and thirst for God. He drinks deep drafts of God's water, his soul burning with God's flame. The monotheism of Israel does not come from the mind but from the heart on fire with the spirit of God. The monotheism of Israel is not an arrival at God's door after a long, slow journey through the paths of reason; on the contrary, it is the result of a soul flinging itself above nature against the door of heaven.

A consciousness of God, such as characterized Israel from the beginning of its history, a consciousness that becomes a living fire, shining, burning, consuming, strongest of the strong—is a fact of revelation. The Most High, who resides in shadows, reveals Himself in a full light. This light demands a continuous reaching of the soul toward God, because faith is finding God in oneself and oneself in God. God cannot sustain loss: He is the eternal Light; but man— man oscillates between God's Light and the world's darkness.

Daily life, earthly life with all its temptations, acts upon the soul with centrifugal force, and the idea of God acts with centripetal force. One can try to silence this interior voice, the articulate need of God who lives and operates in us, but a wind coming from the Lord awakens in us what we would leave slumbering. The soul that has been silent and dying raises a cry, and its awareness of God is alive again. From its depths, the heart raises a voice to heaven, because it sees.

Thus Paul, wounded in his soul, reaches the foot of the Cross. Saul pressed hard after the first Christians in his hatred and was far from Christ; then, caught by Christ's love for him, Saul dies and rises again. Saul dies and rises again in Paul, on fire with love; rich in good works and teaching; ardent and mighty; shining in martyrdom and in the light of Christ, a light that never dies.

Paul is "converted". Did he abandon the God of Israel? Did he cease to love Israel? It would be absurd to think so. But then?

Science is experience preserved, critically evaluated, and methodically expounded; it is empirical par excellence. Starting from sensible experience, it tends to form a hypothesis on the nature of the Absolute. It would be a miserable thing, making the university from year to year like a vast field planted with turnips, unless the Spirit of God who is Truth and life-giving descended there from time to time, for He is the God of all Light.

The scientist, the artisan of culture and of knowledge, prepares himself and his disciples to receive the voice of truth in the same way as the farmer tills the soil: having plowed and seeded it, he awaits the miracle of the sprouting, growing, and ripening of the wheat. In the same way, a saint turns toward heaven to hear the voice of God, to receive the bread of God from the hand of God. Always and everywhere the work is done in preparation for something better, something wholly mysterious.

Agriculture is the bond between the earth and the man who cultivates it; science is the bond between the studious man and scientific truth; religion is the bond between man and God. But religion, as such, is the totality of customs and doctrines by which the religious impulse of a certain epoch in the history of a race was made concrete. *"Religiousness* is precisely the human sentiment eternally *renewing* itself in expressions and forms forever *new*", says Martin Buber, "sentiments of wonder at the existence of the Absolute. . . . It is the desire to bring about a vital communion with this Absolute."

The convert is one who feels impelled by an irresistible force to leave a preestablished order and seek his own proper way. It would be easier to continue along the road he was on.

Mysticism is a potency of religiousness. It reaches further, at the same time remaining the vital nucleus of the religious sphere. As religiousness pulsates life, so mysticism is an uninterrupted pilgrimage toward the Absolute: God. It is a fatiguing and wandering way, lonely and often painful. Mysticism stresses man's need of the infinite. At its highest point, it is a direct contact with the Absolute, the Infinite God. The mystical rapture is a complete annulment of sensible experience; man as such, with the consciousness of his ego, plunges into the Infinite and seems to die. The barriers between him and the Infinite fall. In the mystical rapture, the soul in man is flooded with God and becomes a sanctuary in which God-in-man meets God-in-the-Infinite. The soul "intuitively assimilates" the Infinite.

Religion is religious reality made into an order or system of life. Religiousness is a breathless search for God. Mysticism is a fusion with God. The soul that prays feels according to the relation: I toward Thee; living religiousness is this: I and Thou; mysticism is I, no longer I, in *Thee*. The important thing is to take the road that is yours, chosen, willed by God.

Religiousness renews man and places him on one of the roads leading to God's throne. One can distinguish between the "returned" and the "converted", because each has its own characteristics. The task of religiousness, once it is awakened and made active, is to lead man, the seeker of God *ex novo*, to the road that is his and true. God is truth; He must be loved truly and in truth.

The newly converted need not be praised; still less should he be vituperated and hated. Such a one ought to be loved and understood; loved in that love with which God loves all men.

Conversion is light renewed, love of God renewed. The convert is a man who has died and has risen again. Man, in general, knows God the Creator through creation, through the might of His works. A marvelous documentation of this way of knowing God is Psalm 29 in the original text. The soul, praying, perceives God's voice in the flash of lightning, in the rumble of thunder: the voice that breaks the cedars, makes the mountains tremble, shakes the desert, and fills the wild beasts with fear. The sacred singer knows the Eternal through the "eternity" of time and the "infinity" of space; man serves the just and merciful God in the spirit of justice and piety. He serves Him through obedience to His commandments. The covenant sealed the duty of obedience to the Law and gave to the Chosen People the assurance of divine protection. Thus was the way of man marked.

History presents a grave problem: obedience to the Law, the fulfillment of rites, are for man dangerous virtues, as they give him a sense of self-sufficiency. In love for God there enters also love for the Law, which is divine, but which is not God—just as a masterpiece is an expression of the genius of the artist, without being the artist himself. Love for the Law intrudes on the Law of Love. The empire of the Law often contends with the way to Love's empire. The diagnosis is made by the prophet of the same God who gave the Law, Jeremiah, when he says:

> Behold, the days shall come, saith the Lord, and I will make a *new* covenant with the house of Israel, and with the house of Judah: *not* according to the covenant which I made with their fathers, in the day that I took them by the hand to bring them out of the land of Egypt: the covenant which they made *void*. . . . But *this* shall be the covenant that I will make with the house of Israel. . . . I will give my law in their bowels, and I will write it in their heart: and I will be their God, and they shall be my people. And they shall teach no more every man his brother, saying: *Know* the Lord: for all shall *know* me from the least of them even to the greatest, saith the Lord . . ." (Jer 31:31–34).

The first pact was made after the liberation from Egypt. He who is liberated has the duty of following his liberator, for he belongs to him. I am the Lord who took you out of Egypt, says the Decalogue; hence you shall not have other gods before Me.

The pact was violated. What about the new pact? It will not be written on tables of *stone*; it will be written on the tables of man's heart, that is, in the depths of his *conscience*, which is the source of the knowledge of God, not taught outwardly, but spontaneous and living (Jer 31:3, 33, 34; 32:39, 40). The knowledge of God is not from without, it will spring from within and radiate outward. Man, made new, will feel and know God spontaneously; to man shall belong the duty of making his communion with God more richly satisfying, more vital, closer. The Law teaches and points the way, the running in His way is done by personal volition. To know is to love; we love with our heart and not through notions derived from without.

In Ezekiel 36:25, the language is priestly and the words, although savoring of Levitical ritualism, contain a living flame, an irresistible flood of ardor that breaks through the dikes constructed by the Law. The rite of the purifying water will be accomplished, not by man carrying out an ancient tradition, but by God Himself:

> And I will pour upon you clean water, and you shall be cleansed from all your filthiness, and I will cleanse you from all your idols. And I will give you a *new heart*, and put a *new spirit* within you; and I will take away the stony heart out of your flesh, and will give you a heart of flesh. And I will put My spirit in the midst of you, and I will cause you to walk in My commandments, and to keep My judgments, and to do them. I will cleanse you from all your impurities! (Ezek 36:25, 27, 29).

The very soil will feel the interior renovation of man and will yield abundant fruit. (According to the Old Testament, the earth is contaminated by man's impurities; this concept of the Levitic and prophetic mind is reflected in Pauline thought. While in the sphere of the Mosaic precepts and rites, it is the purifying acts of man that liberate the native soil from the impurity, the prophet looks not for an *exterior* act of man but for a renewal of man himself. The *Lord liberates* man from his impurity, and the renewed interior purity of man acts of itself on the earth.) The Lord renews the *heart* of man by changing it, by making man the temple of the *Divine Spirit.*

Then man *will obey* the Law, but this obedience will be the effect of the *Presence* of the *Spirit of God* in man. The teacher of God's knowledge, and of obedience to the Law, will not be the Law, but the Spirit of God that has become as an integral part of man, the driving force in man. Obedience will correspond to a *motus proprius* of the human heart. The Spirit of God will work in man. While obeying the Law, man will obey what he deems to be his *own* will. Man will have in himself the Spirit of God, and in doing God's will, he will do his own. Man will obey God in himself.

Knowledge of God will be achieved in man through a knowledge that *goes* from man to man, but the master of each will be his heart and will be in his heart. "I will give them", says Jeremiah, "a heart [a heart and not a taught Law] to know Me, who am the Lord; they will be My people, and I will be their God, because they shall *be converted unto Me with all their heart*" (24:7). Man-centricism will give place to Theo-centricism; obedience to God's Law will be pure love of God, thanks to the Spirit of God in man.

This burning expectation of the new manifestation of the Spirit of God in man is accentuated in the prophet Joel. Upon man renewed, upon the renewed soil made fertile, there shall descend abundantly the blessings of the Spirit. "And it shall come to pass after this, that I will pour out My spirit upon all flesh: and your sons and your daughters shall prophesy; your old men shall dream dreams, and your young men shall see visions. Moreover upon My servants

and handmaids in those days I will pour forth My spirit"
(Joel 2:28, 29).

Then shall be realized the prophetic word of Isaiah, the
prophet who spoke of the time when the earth would be
filled with the knowledge of God as the waters fill the sea.

All men are God's creatures; the whole creation is God's
work, and all shall be renewed through an outpouring of the
Spirit of God on all men and all things. All shall ascend to
God and shall be free in God; every man shall know that in
him as in every other man there lives only one Spirit making
him happy and holy: the Spirit of God.

This lofty and majestic thought gave wings to the preach-
ing of Saint Paul, but it likewise came to life in the golden
book, the pearl of rabbinical literature, the *Tanna tebe Eliahu*,
which was taught in the school of Elijah the prophet: "I take
as witness heaven and earth; whether a pagan (Gentile) or
Israelite, whether man or woman, servant or handmaid, each
one according to his work, the Holy Spirit rests upon him."[1]
"In Him there is neither Gentile nor Jew, circumcised nor
uncircumcised, barbarian nor Scythian, bond nor free. But
Christ is all and in all" (Col 3:11).

The doctrine of change of *heart*, of the divine sprinkling
that makes man free from sin—of the Spirit of God poured
out equally on all, free or slave without any difference whatsoever, because all are free from sin—this doctrine is one of
the most marvelous pages in the history of pedagogy. It is not
man who teaches another man to *know* and to love God, to
be grateful to God, but one and the same Spirit: the Spirit of
God, operative, liberating, vivifying all. All men who com-
pose a community are pilgrims of God, sons of God, brothers in God; all obeying the same God, loving, adoring the

---

[1] *Tanna debe Eliyahu*, ed. by Friedmann, p. 48.

same God. Teacher and disciples, priest, prophet, people, all are children of God; this means the spiritual elevation of all, not lessening but increasing the dignity and spirituality of all, the reciprocal understanding of all. *All*, teachers and disciples, are part of the great edifice God is building on earth. All shall know God.

During this period, I made a trip to Palestine, with the help of the Ministry, which gave me economic assistance and a diplomatic pass. On the boat, I became acquainted with a very intelligent Pole, the son of an admiral of the Russian fleet. He was going to Palestine in order to learn something about the country where so many Jews sought refuge. In his company I visited Alexandria, where I gave some lectures for the Jewish Community. In the museum at Cairo, I worked on the Sinaitic inscriptions (so called because they were discovered near Mount Sinai; there is to date no certainty with regard to their interpretation). I made a few photographs, some of which I later published in a magazine for historical and religious studies under the direction of Professor Pettazzoni of the University of Rome, *Studi e Materiali di Storia delle Religioni*. One of my photographs especially proved useful, since it showed that certain signs that had been interpreted as letters were simply the products of rock erosion.

My travel in Palestine was both interesting and instructive. Particularly interesting was my stay in Jerusalem, where I spent much time with Chief Rabbi Cook, whom I had already gotten to know in Trieste. I became acquainted with Meir Lipschuetz, then the director of the pedagogical seminary; with Professor Mayer of the School of Archaeology, with whom I had some very interesting meetings; and with Professor W. Schubert of the University of Berlin, one of the noblest and most generous minds in the university world. He had already done much to facilitate my research in the Cairo museum.

On my return to Italy, I was invited to give some lectures on my impressions of Palestine. These lectures proved to be of interest to Christians as well as Jews, and on one occasion the audience was so large that I could hardly get to the platform.

It was perhaps the success of these lectures that suggested to a certain newspaperman the notion of publishing a few articles on his own impressions of Palestine. He read the Baedecker, added a few imaginative details, and his articles began to appear. So great was the interest in Palestine at that moment, that the articles became very popular, and the writer was encouraged to continue with them. One morning the Secretary of the Hebrew Community approached me saying: "You missed the most interesting thing in Palestine —or, at least, you did not tell us about it." And he handed me an issue of the newspaper with one of the articles in it, which began like this: "Dawn was approaching, the sky was pale. . . . I had an early breakfast, because it was a very important day. The first item on our program was a visit to the tomb of Yahweh."

For us Yahweh is the Eternal Father. What He was in the view of that writer is something I have always wondered about.

From the time of my return from the East until my nomination as Head Rabbi and Director of the Rabbinical College in Rome at the end of 1938, the ferment in my spiritual life was becoming ever more intense. In this pilgrimage, this breathless search, within myself, I wanted to find God, and myself in His presence. I have marked a few points of reference, so as not to lose myself in the maze of my thoughts.

Moses prayed to God: "Show me Thy majesty!" To see in order to know: the two verbs are almost binomial: to see and to know. To *see*, of course, with the eyes of the Spirit. God's answer is disconcerting: "A man cannot see Me and live." Must he die, then? "You will see Me when I shall have passed and made known to you My name."

With fine intuition the ancient doctors have expressed in a form, bold and dangerous yet marvelously true, the meaning of God's word: "The Lord wrapped Himself in a mantle, in a veil that is worn in prayer [the sacred veil that envelops the head of him who prays, symbolically veiling him from the world—an idea alive in Islamism and also among Maronite priests today], and prayed." The Lord taught Moses to pray in this way. Yes, I thought to myself, the Lord, the breath of God, passes before you; you do not see His features, as Job says; you do not take hold of Him; but the Lord teaches you how to pray, and in prayer you see and know your Lord.

How sublime all this is! Nostalgia, love, are excellent ways of knowing. If you love and know Him, you will love well; otherwise, you will be like a moth around a flame, which falls impotent, with singed wings. You have known, and knowing marks your death. Love God, and the more you love Him, the better you will know Him; the more you know Him, the more you will love Him. *He who loves, learns to know;* and he who knows, loves and sees.

And the Lord gives man a heart (this, for orientals, means intellect, intelligence, affective capacity, will) that he may understand God, follow His ways, fulfill His precepts.

Understand in order to love. And Saint John? Love in order to understand. In the precepts of the Pentateuch, the spirit of the Law prevails over the law of the Spirit. In Deuteronomy and in the prophets, the opposite takes place: the empire of the Spirit dominates. Saint John's thought can be summed up thus: He who follows in the Lord's footsteps, he who lives as Jesus lived, he who observes the word of God, loves God, and is in possession of the perfect love of God, he lives in God. He who walks on the way marked by God's steps, dwells in God.

If you know that God is just, you know that anyone who is just is born of God. And the rabbis, jealous for God's attributes, say: As God is clement and merciful, be you also clement and merciful.

"Christ", says Saint John, "was without sin; he who dwells in Him sins not." "He who dwells in fraternal love dwells in God and God dwells in him", says Père Boisnard. The love of God includes the love of man. Why do men not know how to love? The love of man for his Creator supposes the love for every other man. God in man and man in God, all through one sole love. Man cannot see God, but the way for communing with God is open to all. This is Jesus' teaching, developed, brought nearer. He who loves the Lord and loves his neighbor is close to the Kingdom of God.

What about one who loves only God and neglects the love of his brother? Can the love of God be associated with neglect in loving one's brother? Deliberately to humiliate or afflict a brother, and at the same time contribute to an institute of public charity; how can the love of God, then, be one with love for man? And yet—"If we love one another", continues Saint John, "God dwells in us and His love is perfect in us."

This teaching is of a disconcerting reality, cleaving the

flesh and piercing the heart. Is not fraternal charity of the same species as divine charity? "Is not", as the proverb says, "the soul of man like a lamp of the Lord?" Do you not extinguish God's light, you who wound, betray, humiliate, and repel the love that burns for you in the heart of your brother, who loves you in perfect humility and submission?

According to Saint John, he who lives exteriorly, according to the world, is not born of God, for he lives outside of God. God is not in him, and he is not in God. What a terrible realism there is, I said to myself, in these gentle words of Saint John; who knows if Christ's followers are aware of their meaning, of the vigor and rigor of God's law: Love? What becomes of the man who does not love God and his brother at the same time? What is he in God's eyes?

And yet—so it is, and so it must be; this is absolute truth —limpid, vivifying, one and unique.

In the light of the Gospel, the eyes of Saint Augustine and Saint Francis were opened; both drew from the source that springs from the heart and mind of Saint John. Saint Augustine wrote a moving page exalting the beauty of a worm; and Saint Francis stooped to pick up a worm on the road and place it gently on the grass. "Lord", I asked, "if Your servants are merciful even to worms—Saint Francis kissing a leper, Saint Catherine tenderly touching the sores of the sick, Saint Cajetan, following in the footsteps of Saint Francis, making himself the apostle of the incurable—if these saints have known how to interpret and to live the words of the Psalmist: 'His mercy is upon all creatures,' why is there so much pride and incalculable hardness of heart? How has it come to pass that so deep an abyss has opened between the past and the present of the same Christian people? What is the way that leads back to the ancient splendor of Your Holy Spirit?''

Can we live on the brink of an abyss, without a past, without a future? Without a yesterday or a tomorrow? Thick darkness filled my soul, and this very darkness became a prayer. On his deathbed Goethe, who had become blind, uttered these words: "More light!" And within me was heard, as it were, a groan, an invocation hardly formulated: A little more light.

Twenty years have passed since then. Lately I ran across another thought of Boisnard's in my reading: "John was not a Greek (philosopher); he was an Israelite living by the breath of the Spirit."

10. Before the Dawn

The Law of God and the law of the heart: are they in contradiction to each other? No; the Law of God cannot be opposed to the law of the human heart, because the human heart is also God's creation. The Law of God takes in the whole man, soul and body: "All my bones are numbered, all the forces within me, all that lives and works in me", says the Divine Singer. "Lord, who is like unto Thee?" No one is like unto God, because no one outside of God is the All, and man, this diminutive but exceptional *participant of the All*, feels a nostalgia for the All, for Him *who is*; and man knows that *He is*. Therefore man feels continually drawn to the *Being of God*.

For man to flee from God is a vain thing; it is like living under a false name with the illusion of being in reality someone else. This would be tragic childishness, and obviously grotesque. I felt this, I felt it during the period of which I am speaking. I now feel it more than ever.

I understand a little bit of the thought of the great ascetics, although they live in a world inaccessible to me. I felt, and still feel, that God does not take me by force or by surprise, but He calls me and wants me. I call Him, I want Him, I love Him; I am hungry and thirsty for Him. My interior life is not static but is energized by the goal toward which it is directed; I walk on the road of life, toward the land of life. When we walk alone (and one does walk alone toward God), we become one with the road. In the hour of rest, we look around us, and toward the horizon; we think of the

distance covered and all that is still to be done. On the road
that leads to God, we are conscious of the Infinite, like a
rush of wings, because anyone who goes out to meet God
is aware of God's movement toward him. He who walks
toward God knows that the end of one stage is the beginning of another, and still another.

Every morning God is new; He is a God in whom man
renews himself endlessly. Man is a pilgrim toward God, and
the way between God and man is the way of man and God,
because it is the way to God. And thus I was becoming ever
more acutely aware of the *way* on which I was walking. I
find no clearer expression of my feeling, although I know
that even though very ancient, it is not very clear. I often
stumbled over a stone, a thorn would prick my foot, and
sometimes (these were the loveliest hours), on my knees and
with my eyes turned to heaven, I said with tears, "Lord, see,
I walk, I am alone; I will continue to walk, but do You be
my guide, Lord."

One day I saw a long double file of people standing in
the rain, waiting for the doors of a second-class movie the-
ater to open. "Look," I said to myself, "these poor people
have worked steadily for six days, and today they are waiting in the rain to give away part of the fruit of their labor.
They are good people, but they feel the monotony and the
emptiness of life and look for some diversion. They want
to live an hour or two in the illusion of sharing, in thought,
some adventure of love or comic interlude, some thrilling
escapade or mystery." Further along the street was a little
church, silent and empty. There I stood in the rain, under
a gray sky, waiting at God's door.

I felt, and those people did too, that we should plunge
deeper into life, into a fuller, richer life, rich in personal

experience. All—they and I—are hungry, with a hunger that drives us to leave our home and to walk the streets in search of something.

I am a beggar at God's door. I have nothing with which to pay for my admission. Outside my poverty, I have nothing. Those with generous hearts can, without knowing it perhaps, leave some thing of beauty before God's throne. They themselves are a gift they make to God. But I? I am indeed one of those of whom Saint Augustine speaks: "What can man offer to God? Everything in man is from God, only man's sins are his own." And so?

Then I said to myself: Why do you wait, what are you waiting for? Suppose the door should open—would you not say: "Lord, until now I have neglected my soul's misery, sins and failings are all that belong to me; I am weary and footsore"?

No, I must reexamine the path on which I walk and ask myself if it is the true one, the shortest, however difficult this may be. If others stop at the movies to lose precious time, they too will one day appear before You; I must not linger. The sky is gray; it is raining; the wind is cold. I must be attentive to the *way*, it is my friend.

The problem was this: the Law or the law of Love; love of the Law or the law of Love. And this was my solution: the frigidity of a law, of *any law*, is tempered only by the warm rays of love.

I feel the duty of making a confession: the labor of my spirit was along straight lines, but it was nonetheless fatiguing. Never did I think of asking help from anyone. I was convinced that I had to go through it alone. It would have been difficult for anyone to understand me, since I myself was unable to speak of what was going on in my soul. But yielding, unconsciously perhaps, to an irresistible need of stopping, of resting, I spent periods of distraction before resuming my way.

Then a complex array of facts would take hold on my mind, facts that I could describe only with the words: the earth. Was it evil? Was it good? I could not say, but these periods of rest enriched me with a great experience of inestimable value. God was speaking from afar to my soul.

He was calling me. It is unbelievable, and yet it is so. When a man seeks God and tries to be near Him, he feels, sometimes, as if he were standing before a closed door. When he tires of waiting, he tries to get away and to lose himself in the variety that earth offers; nevertheless, he hears God calling him. Man walks in the way of God, whether he remains with God or seemingly leaves Him to do His work. This is the experience I have tried to describe in my article which I called "The Return Road".

Here is a résumé of my experience as I felt it then. At the beginning was God, God alone, with indescribable light and might, with radiant beauty, and infinite wisdom.

He began the work of Creation, the work of the six days. When Creation was finished, then the living, loving, becoming, suffering, enjoying, falling, rising, dying of all created things knew no end. The oneness of might, of beauty, of divine salvation emitted a very great number of luminous rays. To each being that lives, loves, suffers, falls, and rises, God imparted one of His rays. Thus God is united to all creatures because He holds in His hand all these rays, directed everywhere, whose extreme ends reach into the hearts of all men.

God sent out these rays to adorn, enliven and ennoble an "infinite" number of beings, but He follows each radiant thread with a gaze full of grace and charity; His ear bends often to hear their vibrations like sounding chords, to receive the harmonious concerts of the multiplicity of life circulating throughout the universe.

Is man constantly aware of the thread that binds him to his God? Is he always conscious of the luminous reflex of the ray that trembles in his heart?

Alas, very often man loses touch with that resplendent ray, he wanders like a vagabond through the world in search of wealth and power; he loses himself in obscure lands where reign strife, hatred, and envy. His thought is not satisfied with eternal truth, with the sweet flame that warmed and brightened his childhood and adolescence; it is now plunging him into abstruse and devious ways that lead him far astray.

Then God, who holds tight in His hand all the luminous rays that connect Him with His creatures, feels in one of them the painful vibration of a desperate struggle. One more pull—and the soul to whom He is bound thinks himself free, secure, proud. But a fiber of light is tenacious: it can endure tension and tumult; it yields, stretches, is drawn so fine as to become almost imperceptible, but it resists.

Sometimes there comes to one who has tried to detach himself from God a period of depression, of lassitude. His strength seems exhausted. His companions have left him; he is alone, bewildered, and without love. He no longer understands the meaning of life; no longer remembers from whence he comes or whither he goes. Gradually, the consciousness of error awakens in him; he reflects, he thinks back over the steps he has taken, which have led him thus far. Unnoticed there begins to dawn in him a faint light; it is a luminous ray that takes on vigor and energy. His tired soul perceives it faintly at first; he is restless and in doubt. But soon the soul takes desperate hold of it, allows itself to be swayed and carried away, and from height to height is led into marvelous spheres. There the soul is no longer alone; other souls are held in the same hand, the bond of brotherhood strengthens it.

In the thrill of that vision, the soul hears a voice that says: "I did send you out into the world's highways, but My ray of light has never abandoned you. When I saw you going astray, I was here waiting for your return. I waited for the awakening and strengthening of your consciousness of the indissoluble communion between you and Me. Today you return after a long time, perhaps too long a time, but I receive you with a love that is not lessened or overcome. How is it that you did not see that the meaning of life is exactly a continual returning to Me? What is life worth if man gives up the privilege of being God's pilgrim? Your task, the task I entrust to all souls, is to go far, to sow everywhere wisdom and charity. But you must remain always and everywhere conscious of your divine origin, son of your Father in heaven, who is One and Unique. The noise of life must never drown out the sound of the heavenly harmonies within you."

In the Christmas season, the Hebrews have a feast, the characteristic rite of which consists in lighting candles and other lights. On the first night one candle is lighted, the next night another, and so on until there are eight. This is the feast of the heroic Maccabees. No one can tell with certainty the origin and meaning of the feast, but all know that these heroes are the embodiment of the courageous defense of the liberty to adore God. They rose against the oppressor and knew no peace, nor did they turn away from battle and death, until they had liberated their country from slavery; they defended their faith in the one true God.

Their heroism was refined by martyrdom. A hero is a

martyr in action. The martyr is a hero in suffering and sorrow carried unto passion and death. The martyr and hero are the synthesis of an ideal, and of sacrifice for that ideal, in one and the same person.

In our times, heroism is spoken of in cases when violence is done in the name of a "chosen race", of a nationalism that is absolute and excessive, condemned by the wise, profound, and incisive words of Pope Pius XII:

> For those who have allowed themselves to be seduced by the instigators of violence, and after having unwisely followed them, begin now to awake from their illusion, astonished to see how far their servile docility has led them—for them, there is no other way of salvation than to repudiate definitely the idolatry of absolute nationalism, pride of race and blood, the craving for earthly possessions, and to turn resolutely to the spirit of sincere brotherhood, founded on the cult of the Divine Fatherhood of all men, in which cult the concepts, too long opposed, of rights and duties, of advantages and of burdens, harmonize with justice and charity (Allocution of His Holiness Pius XII to the faithful, Passion Sunday, 1945).

The patriotism of the Maccabees was different from the kind that culminates in a slaughter of the innocents. Saint Augustine made himself the interpreter of the nobility of the struggle sustained by the Maccabees, in Latin words I hardly dare to translate, for fear that in so doing I should damage them, as one injures the delicate wings of a butterfly or the petals of a flower:

> *Idem ipsi fuit Deus trium puerorum, qui fuit Machabeorum. Illi de igne evaserunt, illi ignibus cruciati sunt, utrique tamen in Deo sempiterno vicerunt.* It was the same God of the three children in the fiery furnace, who was the God of the Maccabees; those were saved from fire, these suffered martyrdom by fire; both won the victory in the Eternal God.

I dare not add a word; I can only report something that was intimated to me one day—or, rather, one evening—many years ago, by a flame of the *hanukkah*, by one of those candles destined to preserve and transmit the memory of the achievements of the Maccabees.

In my family—I do not know why—there was the tradition of lighting candles instead of the hanukkah lamp, which burns by oil. We were on the fourth evening of the feast. Before me was a scarlet candle, beside it one of orange hue, a third of white, and a fourth blue like the sky. The little flames were beautiful, and they filled us with joy when they began to burn well in all their vigor. But I remember that, child though I was, I felt something like desolation enter my heart when the little flames, having done their task, began to flicker, leap, sink, and flare up again; in a word; as they began to struggle between life and death. I stared at the dying lights in half-conscious fascination and with a sense of melancholy.

More than sixty years have passed since I lost the pleasure of being a child; yet I remember how that evening I raised my eyes to the hanukkah and saw that the scarlet candle had died. From the orange one, a thin curl of smoke was mounting and spreading out like a flower; it trembled and then vanished. So this candle also went out. Shortly after, the white candle began to fight for its existence, and then died. The blue was left, recalling heaven to me; it lasted longer. We were alone, the flame and I; it spoke to my heart—the heart of a child is so much more sensitive than the hearts of grown-ups. It said: "I understand you, I look within you, I know what you think. You share my spasms with sorrow; you follow with sympathy every movement of mine toward heaven, and every sinking of mine into obscurity. It is not in vain that you are called Israel; he who fought for something divine. Do not feel sad for me—I die gladly. Moreover, I know that I did not come here to serve a selfish cause. I and all my sisters, the flames of hanukkah, serve a great ideal. To live for an ideal is beautiful. But to die for an ideal is beautiful, enviable, pleasing, a desirable thing; perhaps it is even desired. Do you believe", continued the tiny light in the dark, "that it is only in this room that the flames of hanukkah are burning and shining? No, we are millions, scattered all over the world, in the cold lands of the north and the warm lands of the south; in the homes of the poor and the palaces of the rich; even on the ships that cross the seas, carrying Hebrews to their country. Everywhere we give our life in memory of the struggle of Israel for his existence, his liberty of conscience, his ideals. You know in how many places, in how many lands, under how many skies the spirituality of the Jews is repressed, the inner light of Israel extinguished? Well, in times of sorrow as in times of joy, we, the little flames of the hanukkah, come quietly, serene and gentle, into the temples and the homes of the Hebrews to declare everywhere a great truth: 'The Light of Israel cannot, must not be put out; it always revives because the soul of Israel is undying.'"

The candle was still; it seemed to have thrown up its last splash of light, but the memory of it illumined my heart: "Remember well, that he is free who grants others their liberty, and he who aims only at his own freedom falls into the pit of his own egotism. No one may demand liberty for himself who holds others as slaves. See, child, how carefully your mother always prepares us, and with how much delicacy she chooses our colors. And before us your father recites the blessing and the psalm, and your eyes are delighted with our flames. But a day will come when you will understand more through meditation. I tell you now: the Encenia[1]

---

[1] This is the Greek name of the feast.

lamp must be taken as a whole, as a unit, regardless of the diversity of colors and the divers length of times we candles last. Outside the unity of God, every unity is multiple, it is composed of millions of beings bound together. Do you truly think that a drop of water is an absolute and simple unity? Do you know that your eye, which enjoys the light of the sun, is itself endowed with solarity? Take from the eye its solarity, and you will have a broken instrument, torn, impoverished, dead. Look at a drop of dew on a blade of grass in a meadow; it shines like fire, it resembles a miniature sun on a shining green background. Oh, no, my child, you must not stop at the surface; you must learn how to perceive the vibrations of all that lives. I am only a simple candle, but I am part of a hanukkah that expects a blessing and a song, as you also are a lamp destined to hold many lights, and to perpetuate the will of God, the source of infinite vibrations within many living beings. In you also, many lights will shine; whether you will or not, they will die out, but you will always be a living lamp and new light will be kindled in you.

"Do you know why I call you *ante lucem*? It is a Latin term which means 'the vigil of light'—that is, *before the dawn*. At the hour of your death, when it will seem as if the last light has gone out within you, upon you and in you will dawn a great light: the great Light of God!"

At this a thin tongue of flame showed itself momentarily in silence. It was the last flicker of the blue candle.

11. Is Conversion an Infidelity?

My thought runs to the Epistle of Saint Paul to the Romans and to those unforgettable words: "I speak the truth in Christ, I lie not, my conscience bearing me witness in the Holy Ghost: that I have great sadness, and continual sorrow in my heart. For I wished myself to be an anathema from Christ, for my brethren, who are my kinsmen according to the flesh, who are Israelites" (Rom 9:1–4). Here is how Eric Peterson comments on the last sentence of this passage:

> The moving exaltation is at its apex, intense sorrow seeks a supreme expression. Paul wished on himself the anathema, through love of his brethren, of Israelite kinsmen. He never wearies of calling them with new names. We feel how attached Paul is to his people in all his existence: morally, physically and religiously. For Saint Paul, the relations between the Synagogue and the Church are a problem of existence.

The dominant note in the psychology of the Apostle is that of a great love that never falters, even in face of the most extreme consequences. The dazzling light on the road to Damascus kindles the fire that burns in the soul of Saul and consumes it. He, Saul, is dead. When he rises, he is crucified to the world, and the world is crucified to him; his soul, his life from now on, are Jesus Christ. Saul becomes Paul, and even Paul lives no longer: Christ lives in him. His vehement love, lived by him to its uttermost consequences, does not turn away from any sacrifice, no matter how great it may be. He wishes to be freed even from the frail body that wraps the sacred flame within him, because it is a body of death. Here he is, ready to give up his bond with Christ for the salvation of Israel, the Israel of God. Israel must ascend! Israel that has seen a cross erected must acknowledge, love, and adore this cross, the Cross of Christ.

How heroic, I dare to say how tragic, is the psychology of the saints! Saint Francis Xavier would accept eternal condemnation, provided he could increase God's glory; and Saint Paul is willing to be cut off from Christ for the sake of Christ. The Apostle had an unlimited love of liberty, and can anyone be free unless he is the servant and follower of Christ?

The teachers of the Law used to say: liberty is engraved on the tables of the Law. No one is free but the man who sits studying the Law. Justice, which is justification, is the Law. And Paul wanted to see the law of love flourish instead of love for the Law. The Law in opposition to *"faith working through charity"* is like Hagar the slave; Sinai, a mount in Arabia, has great resemblance to the actual Jerusalem, a slave with her children. But the Jerusalem from above, which is free, is our mother. A mother loves and is loved. Christ did not die in vain. The Jerusalem from above, the Church, is Christ-Love. When we love, we live Christ. The Spirit proceeds again and again from love. The Law without love is sterile and generates slaves. He who obeys love follows a loving impulse that is creative, conferring joy and blessedness. Love of God and of Christ is supreme law. Love is a law to itself. Love is living, ever more vigorous, endowed with an unlimited moral power, ever renewed and strengthened.

Law often acts from the outside toward the center; love starts from the center. The Law is teaching; it marks the way. Christ-Love is the Way, the Life, the Light. A man can be deflected from the way of the Law, if charity does not give him life. But there is no deflection from the law of Love, provided it is kept ardent and true. One may obey the Law and remain correct, but cold in the soul. Love, as long as it is true, is light and warmth; darkness and cold cannot enter where Love burns.

The Law, when cleverly handled, can condemn and send an innocent man to his death. The Law requires light and love to carry out its mission. With the exterior only of the Law, a saint can be condemned to death: one of those saints born of love, grown up in love, who dies for love.

When love is placed in the center, it becomes law, holy and gloriously operative; hence Saint Paul is ready, because of love, to accept all sacrifices, if thereby he can give to Israel, those people of the Law, the greater law of Love. And every Christian, every brother of Jesus Christ, must sow love in the soul of Israel, Israel wounded and bleeding. Only he who sows charity causes that faith which works through charity to germinate, and God is Charity.

Typology — for Ecumenism

Is conversion an infidelity, an infidelity toward the faith previously professed? To answer hurriedly yes or no would not be just; too much zeal would be displayed one way or the other, and too much zeal is notoriously harmful. Before answering, one should stop and ask himself what *faith* is in itself. Faith is an adherence, not to a tradition or family or tribe, or even nation, it is an adherence of our life and our works to the *will* of God as it is revealed to each in the intimacy of conscience. Was Saint Paul unfaithful? How many Christian Jews he had cast into prison! How merciless he was against his brothers, who were guilty only of having accepted the message of Christ.

But the Spirit of God breathes where He wills and how He wills. One day the rumor went abroad in Trieste, where

I was Head Rabbi, that one of the most diligent and zealous councillors of the Community, Professor David Guido
Nacamuli, who later died in America, had become a Christian—a Catholic. After a few days, he himself informed me
of it in a letter in which he thanked God for the friendship
we had had for each other and asked me if I were disposed
to continue it. I made an affirmative reply by phone. Half an
hour later he came to see me; we spoke for an hour of many
serious matters without touching the subject of his conversion. Had he asked for my opinion, I would have replied
that to an intelligent man and a fervent Hebrew such as he
had been (he was in addition, an ardent Zionist), conversion
meant obedience to the voice of conscience.

The Jews who are becoming converts today, as in the days
of Saint Paul, have much, or even all, to lose in regard to
earthly life, and have much, if not all, to gain in the life of
grace. The times have passed when a bishop, or a patrician,
or a prince would take a convert under his wing. A few
years ago I met here in Rome, on the steps of the Piazza
della Pilotta, a young Hebrew of the people. He and his
family—wife and children—had become Christians several
years before the race persecution. "We are happy", he said,
"but I do not succeed in finding work. The bread and soup
that are given me daily in a convent do not suffice. We are
many in my family!"

I asked, "What kind of work are you looking for?"

He replied, "I would like to be a shoe-shiner and a porter
in a hotel, even a second-class one." Was ambition the motive of this man's conversion? The answer is clear. About ten
days later I met him again. "How is everything?" I asked.

"Very well indeed", he replied. "I found the work I
wanted."

It is sometimes charged that "converts seek to free themselves from the yoke of the Law, that is from 'works'." Is the small number of converts *nonobservant*? Is Christianity making an easy way through faith without works? There are works of a different kind; but there are plenty of "works", and Christian teaching issues a strong call to works.

Jesus said: "Not every one that saith to Me, Lord, Lord, shall enter into the kingdom of heaven, but he that doth the will of My Father who is in heaven, he shall enter into the kingdom of heaven" (Mt 7:21). "Whosoever shall do the will of My Father that is in heaven, he is My brother, and sister, and mother" (Mt 12:50).

"What shall it profit, my brethren, if a man say he hath faith, but hath not works?" says Saint James (2:14).

> Faith, if it have not works, is dead in itself (2:17).

> Do you see that by works a man is justified, and not by faith only? (2:24).

> Be ye doers of the word and not hearers only, deceiving your own selves. For if a man be a hearer of the word and not a doer, he shall be compared to a man beholding his own countenance in a glass. For he beheld himself and went his way, and presently forgot what manner of man he was. But he that hath looked into the perfect law of liberty and hath continued therein, not becoming a forgetful hearer but a doer of the work: this man shall be blessed in his deed (1:22–25).

Does the convert advance in the hierarchy of social life? The great prisoner of the Lord, Saint Paul, says:

> Do nothing for party spirit or vainglory; let everyone in all humility consider the others as superior to himself; let everyone seek not his own interest but that of others.

> Let no evil word come from your mouth . . . put away anger, indignation, malice, injury and all wickedness. . . . Bearing

with one another, and forgiving one another. . . . even as the
Lord has forgiven you. But above all these things have charity, which is the bond of perfection. . . . Wives be subject to
your husbands . . . children obey your parents. . . . Servants
obey in all things your masters according to the flesh.

One learns how to be free in God even though one be a
slave.

Onesimus, the fugitive slave, robbed his master, a rich
Christian of Colossa, a friend of Saint Paul. The slave, converted by Saint Paul in Rome, was freely returned to his
place of servitude, carrying with him a priceless treasure: a
brief letter from Saint Paul. In it the Apostle said:

> Though I might well make bold in Christ to prescribe a duty
> to thee, I prefer to appeal to this charity of thine. Who is it
> that writes to thee? Paul, an old man now, and in these days
> the prisoner, too, of Jesus Christ; and I am appealing to thee
> on behalf of Onesimus, the child of my imprisonment. . . .
> I am sending him back to thee; make him welcome, for my
> heart goes with him (Philem 8–12).

Saint Paul wanted the benefit of Onesimus' liberation by
Philemon to be not forced but voluntary; he wished the
master to receive the slave as a most dear brother. He who
liberates and he who is liberated must obey—and it is hard
obedience for Onesimus—the voice of Christ whose servants we all are, in whom all are free and elevated through
humility.

What is asked of the Christian? No easy thing. Hear Saint
Paul again: "Bless them that persecute you; bless and curse
not. . . . Not minding high things, but consenting to the
humble. Be not wise in your own conceit. Render to no
man evil for evil. . . . Be not solicitous in anything. . . .
And the peace of God which surpasses all understanding

will keep your hearts and minds in Christ Jesus." As he said, so he lived, and in the name of what he said and lived; he died shedding his blood: he, Paul, the converted Jew.

Unconsciously, quite unconsciously, I was beginning to find in Christianity a springtime of the spirit, full of the expectation of new life made eternal; Christianity represented for me the object of a longing for a love that should temper my soul's winter, an incomparable beauty that should quench my desire for beauty. My book *The Nazarene* was a glorification of Christianity, which had made itself heard like a song in my soul. In the words of the Song of Songs: "Winter is now past, the rain is over and gone. The flowers have appeared in our land: the time of pruning is come; the voice of the turtle-dove is heard."

The slow preparation for spiritual rebirth is much like the preparation that takes place in nature: all is accomplished in silence, and no sign appears of the wondrous event to come. All of a sudden, it seems, the earth is covered with green and the trees are decked with red and white blossom. Like snow-stars, petals float in the air, and there is promise of fruit. One great biological process has reached completion, and a fresh cycle of life is taking on concrete reality, becoming crystallized. The dying we saw was only apparent; it meant the transformation of the life lived into a new life, a life to be lived.

What seemed to die in me had left in my soul the germs of a new life, the life of Jesus Christ. What seemed to be withdrawing from me was leaving an ineffable desire for renewal. New strengths were awakened; nothing could be perceived; but in the depths of my soul I felt the sadness of one who is alone on the road.

12. Was Christ a Hebrew according to the Flesh?

Mussolini was opposed to the persecution of Jews in Germany, although he was no lover of the Jews, and at times liked to make fun of them and of Hebraism in general. He was a man of little religious sensibility and no religious culture. (Once, for example, he asked Cardinal Schuster whether the dogmas were the same in Rome as in Milan— he meant the liturgical chants.) His opposition to persecution had, as a matter of fact, a chiefly political basis, inasmuch as it would mean a break with American Hebraism and the "banks". Husserl, the German ambassador at Rome, was opposed to anti-Semitism for reasons of a deeper nature.

One day a person whose name cannot be mentioned gave me a long account of inhuman acts perpetrated against Hebrews in Germany. It was written in German, and as the Head Rabbi in Rome was not familiar with this language, I decided to translate it faithfully into Italian. It took me three days, and I spent those days in an almost unbroken fast. Then I sent the whole thing by means of a trusted person to the Rabbi of Rome, with the request that it be presented to Mussolini. The Rabbi replied that already, on past occasions, Mussolini had expressed to him his disapproval of persecutions, but nevertheless he would not fail to present the document to the Head of the Government. And this he did. Later, he wrote: "He looked at the document in my presence; he was saddened and remarked, 'I have always said that if you scratch a German, you find a barbarian! However, I will speak of this to Husserl again."'

This statement about Germans was too sweeping. There were Germans who did all they could to hide and protect the Jews. As long as the procedure was feasible, German priests wearing cassocks, hiding Jews among them, accompanied refugees across the Swiss border. The remark only shows that Signor Mussolini spoke man-to-man in the name of humane feelings.

In Trieste, there was a professor of the History of Art, a Fascist, a Catholic and a man of good life, but a fanatic; he initiated a series of anti-Hebrew conferences in the parochial hall of the Church of Barcola. The eloquence of the orator, added to the current interest in the subject, attracted an ever-growing audience.

The director of the tramways organized an efficient service to and from the place, with an increasing number of cars. The police sent a group of *carabinieri* to keep order. Young Hebrews of every class (some students of the university) were in attendance, certainly not with the simple intention of increasing the number of listeners, already very great; strife was plainly in the air, and there might be violence. I invited the leaders among the youth to come to me and give me the substance of the conferences. The printed programs they showed me were certainly designed to inculcate hatred, but I begged the students to do nothing, but to leave the whole matter to me. That same evening there was a plenary sitting of the Hebrew Community Council, and, as was to be foreseen, all agreed that I and the President should ask for an audience with the Prefect and the Chief of Police. I begged them not to take this step—ties of friendship had bound me for years to each new Prefect who came to Trieste, although now it would seem that things had changed. How could we explain to the Chief of Police why we did not like the conferences, that they were dangerous? It seemed useless. A way must be found. But what? I said, "Let me maneuver by myself. We shall see. We can always make the visit you have planned, but I repeat, it will not help."

The next morning, I went to the Ecclesiastic Administrator, who was acting on an interim appointment as the Episcopal See was vacant. He said, "I scarcely know what to say; the matter depends on the Pastor of Barcola."

I replied, "Why should I go to him, since he is the organizer of the conferences? Is there not another way?"

"You might try the Jesuit Father Petazzi, at the Church of Via Ronco. He is a friend of the lecturer", he said.

"Thank you, Monsignor", I replied.

At the Church in Via Ronco, I was told, "Father Petazzi is making his retreat; he finishes it tomorrow. Of course, he is seeing no one now."

The next conference was scheduled for Sunday, and the program, in my opinion, contained high explosives. Tomorrow meant Friday evening. I answered, "Please greet the Reverend Father for me and tell him to have the Professor come here—I shall arrange to be present at any hour he may wish."

The next day a telephone call came at 8:00 P.M. From the ceremonies in the temple I went straight to the sacristy of the church. I paid my respects to the priest and shook hands with the Professor, who responded rather coldly, taking from a large leather case a number of pamphlets, newspapers, booklets—all anti-Semitic—which he began to read. A whole hour passed, and he was still reading; then I interrupted, saying that the Father (an elderly man) might be tired, and that I must not take advantage of his hospitality. I felt that this material (a small library) demanded more time than I had to give. I wanted to ask only one question, and I did so: "Was Christ a Hebrew according to the flesh? Did Christ on the Cross ask pardon for His enemies? How, then", I said, "can a good Catholic hold such conferences without realizing that he is crucifying Christ in spirit, in His holy will, in His teachings? The Jew", I went on, "is not your enemy, nor do I wish to appear an enemy of Christ. God is love. And if God is love, I hope that the day may not come when you have to say to yourself what I would not say, in the spirit of charity, that you are without God.

"One more thing", I added. "I belong to the line of the prophets, and I prophesy to you that the day is not far distant when we shall be friends, because you are fundamentally good, although embittered, and I—I do not think that I am bad. And now, with Father's permission, I will leave."

The Professor, who had listened attentively, was looking at me with a new friendliness. "What shall I do on Sunday?" he now asked. "The conference has already been announced and also the program!"

"Read the Gospel, as I do myself sometimes", I replied. "The rest will take care of itself."

"May I go along with you now?"

"Indeed you may."

So we went out together. It was raining, and there was a strong, cold wind. When we reached the door of my house, we shook hands cordially and parted.

Sunday at noon a university student came from Barcola and reported to me what had happened at the meeting. "The speaker stood up and began by saying that a high Jewish personage had troubled his conscience, and that he did not wish to continue on a path that could never be, for him, the same again. After that he sat down, and said he would lecture on a famous ivory crucifix of the thirteenth century. He ended by saying that the series of conferences [eight more were scheduled] was closed.''

"And then?" I asked.

"Applause and a mad race for a place in the trolley cars", said he.

After dinner an unannounced visitor came to my home. We embraced and gave each other the kiss of peace—and a cup of tea. We were, and still are, friends.

Between the Resurrection and the Ascension, Christ was no longer a part of mankind as He had been before He died on the Cross, in the midst of the insults and the savage cries of the multitude, and the intense love of a few. He was no longer a man like other men, nor was He yet sitting at the right hand of the Father. He was outside this world and not yet in the kingdom that is not of this world.

The wavering faith of Peter was like a flickering torch before becoming a pillar of fire. Lack of faith grieves Jesus. Thomas was still doubting; complete lack of faith in Christ wounds Christ. The glorified Christ waits, listens; still Thomas doubts. Then Christ appears and offers not faith but His wounds. He offers His wounds, hiding in His heart the sadness for him who is alone on the way, the way that leads from earth to heaven, from the Passion to the throne of the Father.

Who is there that does not hide his wounds? And especially from one who doubts?

How different from Christ men are! To those who doubt their strength, sharp weapons are presented, accompanied by sharp looks, with provoking contempt and hatred. Not so, Christ. He presents His holy weapons: sorrow, charity,

and the bleeding wounds of His Passion. It is at the sight of
the wounds that man, cold-hearted and blind, discovers the
warmth of the love and the glory of God which is eternal
light. Jesus Christ speaks to us through His wounds, and
even one who doubts is impelled to say, "My Lord and my
God!" It was the sight and the touching of the wounds of
Christ that made Thomas exclaim, "My Lord and my God!"

Man and Christ meet again and recognize each other in
the light issuing from Christ's wounds. And as Christ met
Thomas, so should man meet man and nation meet nation.
The world wounds and betrays; but let every wound in every other man—a brother in Christ—be the light of love
in Christ. As Christ said to Thomas, so let every man say
to his brother, "May my wounds be light for you"; and let
the other reply, "May my wounds and my love be light for
you."

"Without some degree of justice," said Plato, "not even
a society of thieves could subsist; they must unite to strip
wayfarers." A philosopher of our own time has said, "A
people become a state only through the law, which must
be a moral, positive law." The legislator must not be "the
technical promoter of violence". The law must be promul-
gated in the name of a divine principle, of an eternal moral
truth that, in its specific future realization, expresses respect
not only for the life of men but also for their honor. "Let
the honor of thy neighbor be as dear to thee as thy own",
taught the ancient doctors. There is no liberty where the
legislators and the inhabitants of a country do not obey the
same moral law without distinction of race, nationality, or
religion. Hitlerism expressed the opposite of all this. "The
will of the Führer" of itself is law, held the theorists of that
tragic aberration.

In the Major Temple of Trieste, I severely criticized the Laws of Nuremberg. Shortly afterward I received a letter stamped with the seal of the Party, which had sent a man commissioned to teletype my discourse. The letter expressed thanks for the sincerity with which I had spoken my thoughts. (This letter from the Nazi party in its original was given to the Prefect of Trieste by the Advocate Dompieri, having been sent first to the Minister of the Interior.) Soon afterward I was deprived of my Italian citizenship.

III

Rome

13. Saint Paul's Conscience

The Israelite Community of Rome sent its President to Trieste, to offer me the vacant chair of Head Rabbi and Rector of the Rabbinical College in Rome. In due course, I set out on the journey. In Milan, I met the late Dr. Mario Falco, Professor of Canon Law in the university of that city; as Hebrews, we had both been forced to resign "voluntarily" from our universities, Milan and Padua.

"The Rabbinical College in Rome is the only one in Italy", he said. 'To all intents and purposes it is closed, under key. The students are wandering about the streets, and all the professors have migrated. Do you plan to revive the Institute?" This was a very straightforward speech, and I was perplexed.

The Hebrew Council of Rome was composed of two groups—a larger, which saw the way of salvation in a formal adhesion to the Government, and a "nationalist" minority. Immediately after the first sitting I entreated the representatives of both these parties to disarm, rather than to follow the example of the politics of our forefathers when Jerusalem was besieged by the Roman legions; to dedicate the Council to alleviating the gravity of the hour in an atmosphere outside politics; to take care of worship, religious teaching, and works of mutual assistance. My appeal met with a glacial silence, the meaning of which was, to quote a famous phrase of Badoglio, "The war continues."

The teaching was resumed. Some of the young rabbis of

today were my pupils then. I began by taking part in the cele-
bration of marriages and funerals, even those of the poorest,
wishing to give relief in those sad times to the less happy. I
sought work for the unemployed, whose number was growing with the more severe racial legislation.

One day a representative of poor persons came to me to
make a complaint: "For years we have earned our living by
the sale of picture postcards. We sold them on small stands
that we placed at the most frequented corners of the streets.
Now they chase us away because we are Jews."

I replied, "Do not worry, I will try to help you, and do
you pray the Lord to help me."

On the afternoon of the following day, I went to see the
Minister. He received me with much courtesy; we shook
hands—without the Fascist salute. I had the feeling that I
was dealing with a kind and good person.

"Your Excellency", I said, "I have come to propose to
you the foundation of a society for investments."

"Will it be lucrative?" he asked, under the impression
that it was a joke.

"The investments will be both good and lucrative", I
replied, "if not in this world, certainly in the next."

"I am a practicing Catholic, and I am interested. Who
will be the first to invest?" he inquired.

"You and I", I said.

"What is the aim of this new society?"

"To give back to the Jews of the Ghetto the possibility
of selling their picture postcards", I answered.

"This is a question of Party discipline. I really can do
nothing!" he objected.

"I see", I said. "Discipline is synonymous with justice.
But in Italy, you know, the Ministry is called 'of grace and

justice'. As in religion, so in social life, grace must precede justice."

He raised a few more objections, then said, "Tell them, as advice from me, not to stay fixed in one spot for hours; let them move from one place to another. I shall take care of the rest."

"I see", I answered, looking him straight in the eyes. "We Jews must be *wandering*, even when selling postcards."

The Minister pressed my hand and escorted me through the offices to the head of the stairs.

Some days later I met him in the street. He had someone with him. This time we did not greet one another.

It is not my intention to write the history of the Hebrews in Rome during the years 1943–1944 [in this chapter], but my life, the exterior part at least, is painfully bound up with the events of those days, with the responsibilities that weighed inexorably on the shoulders of the representatives of Roman and Italian Hebraism. Later on, I shall explain at some length why thousands of Jews, especially the unsuspecting ones, were left crowded in the Ghetto, to be sent like sheep to the slaughter. I must say now, in the interest of truth and not of self-defense, that I do not give a thought to men's judgments: God knows all.

In the period of the German occupation of Rome, non-Roman (and non-Italian) influences were noticeable in the Roman Jewish Community. A crisis was brought about that overthrew the government of the Community in the last months of Fascism. A strong Hebrew government was formed, favorable to the Government of the nation; but at the same time, preparations were made for evolution into a body both anti-Fascist and National-Hebrew.

As for me, I was beginning to yield, while awaiting the post-Fascist period. The foundations of Fascism were shaken by the events of the war; no one doubted the coming of an Allied victory and the fall of Fascism. The Fascists also were aware of the impending end, and waxed more violent and greedy. The worst elements quickly came to the fore.

The same Fascist Government that had deprived me of Italian citizenship, in practice seemed to ignore me and gave me no trouble. I was asking for nothing. However, certain elements of the Community Council wished to take advantage of my loss of citizenship. A rabbi without a city? Never. The contract was to be modified at my expense. "Let this period pass", I said. "Before the end of it, all of us will be declared expatriates!" This "prophecy" came true, inasmuch as the republic of Salò declared "expelled" all the Jews of Italy and confiscated their goods. Nevertheless, the moment seemed to them propitious for their action against me, and this work was carried on more hastily in view of the impending liberation. I was to be crushed *now*, not so much for the present as for the future. I retired from the scene of battle. I would not oppose them. I realized that it was now no longer a battle of justice against injustice, but between conscience and conscience.

Two differing consciences were opposed. I withdrew into myself to meditate upon the subject of conscience. I started to examine the problem in the light of Pauline doctrine. It did not appear to me to be a case of conversion on my part; I only wished to find the source of the pattern of my own conscience, so different from that of these others. But I had all my life been aware of the difference between the two types of consciences. The conscience of others, so very different from mine, I began to look upon as a failure in the exercise of the conscience. But what is conscience? I was convinced that conscience was the *nervus rerum*, the vital nucleus, not only of the whole life of the individual, but of all human activity, of all human history, including the tragic period through which we were then passing and the worst war of history.

I wanted to study the problem of conscience in Saint Paul because his doctrine appeared to me to be fundamental in the history of the complete development of the human conscience. Here are my findings: We start from the law written in the human heart and proceed to the natural law; to this another factor is added, both human and divine, man's conscience and intellect, taking up the task of interiorly judging man himself; in his interior, accusation and defense are followed by a verdict.

The way of men who possess a written law is different; starting from this written law, they run the risk of becoming whisperers, studious reciters, executors of the Law, devoid of a *motus proprius* of the spirit.

Conscience is witness of self, knowledge of self. The natural conscience is revealed in what God has inscribed in the heart; the voice of God in man. After that, the reason judges, approving or disapproving.

The Gentiles of whom Saint Paul speaks do not recite the law because they have no written law, but they are not, on this account, without law, for they have a law within themselves, the natural law. It is on this that the Gentiles will be judged: Did they, or did they not, act *according to their law*, in perfect accord with *their* conscience?

They will be justified without written law. To the Hebrews, the Apostle says, "Unlike the Gentiles, you Hebrews have in the Law a formula of knowledge and of truth, a written expression. Therefore if you violate the law given you and formulated by God Himself, you dishonor God."

It is a grievous mistake to stop at the recitation of the Law without concern for observing it. The Gentiles have no texts to recite, and therefore there is no separation between them and the interior reality they have to face at each moment.

If a Hebrew, having the text of the written law, does not follow it, it is fully evident that the Law does not save him from sin, which is death. The Law gives only the theoretical knowledge of sin, but does not defend him from sin. The Law is therefore a means of acquiring knowledge and does not produce justification before God.

Nor do the works of the Law avail. We hold that man is justified by faith, without the works of the Law. Why? Because the works of the Law are nothing but the Law coldly translated without the heart's cooperation. Works are the immediate fruit of obedience to the Law, which Law is light from God's light, but it is written with cold ink on cold parchment. The Law is potential work, the works are law in action; but between the law and the work there exists no interior labor, no interior torment. There is wanting the fire of the human heart which shines and burns, which burns and purifies, which makes man suffer but not die, which opens the door to eternal life.

He who does not live by faith in works as works (it is here that I hope to have caught the intimate thought of Saint Paul), lives by faith, and it is faith that is reputed to justice. He who lives by faith in works expects the reward for his works. He who lives by faith, hopes, expects all, not from his works but from God's grace. We do not scorn works, because faith without works is like a spring with no flowering, autumn without fruit. He who hopes in himself performs works and expects his reward as his due. He also works who does not attribute any value to his works and yet hopes—for he also hopes, but he hopes for God's grace. He who lives by faith hopes, and his hope does not deceive, because charity is shed abroad in our hearts by the Holy Spirit, which is given us.

The love of God is diffused in our hearts by the Holy Spirit, who is a pledge, a promise; grace, which makes us hope, makes us expect all from God's love for us. The Holy Spirit makes us hope in the Love who generates, strengthens our faith in Love Himself and not in the works we have done in the strength of the Law.

Baptized in Christ's death, we are through Him dead to sin, in order to rise to a life in God as servants of God who live for God, for Christ, who knew no sin, and who suffered for our sins, which are our death. Christ died for our sins out of pure love for us.

Is the Law, then, evil? God forbid! The Law is holy; holy and just are the Commandments. But the Law is "spiritual" and I am carnal, and sin has its dwelling in me. This is our tragedy.

Sin has its dwelling in me, and I do not do the good I want to do, but the evil I do not want to do, the evil I hate; because it is not I who am in control but the sin that lives in me. In his spiritual part, man delights in the law of God, but in his lower self is operative a law that is opposed to that of his mind. And so, to the law of my mind is opposed the law in my lower powers, the law of sin and death, and it renders the law of my mind impotent.

What is left to me? Not to follow the wisdom of the flesh,

which is death and which annuls the holy and spiritual law of love, of faith through love. The wisdom of the flesh cannot be subject to the law of God who is love; it is an enemy of God and love. But if Christ is in us, then our body of sin is dead and we live according to the wisdom of the Spirit of God which is in us, because Christ is in us: and we live according to the wisdom of the Spirit who is *life* and *peace*.

We live, we who have the first fruits of the Spirit—a thought that is so dear to Saint James; also we hope in things not seen (for hope is not concerned with what can be seen). We live by faith in the love of God; by the love of Christ for us; and without Him we can do nothing. Of ourselves, we cannot even pray as we ought, but the Holy Spirit Himself pleads for us with unutterable groanings. He who reads the heart knows what the Spirit desires; He intercedes for the saints in conformity with the will of God.

Saint Paul's conscience and the nobility of his character shine fully in the words in which he expresses his sorrow for Israel's unbelief. "I speak the truth in Christ", he says, and his grief carries him to the length of exclaiming, "I wish myself to be an anathema from Christ for my brethren!"

Having finished my analysis, I felt refreshed in spirit. I found in myself a reflex, however faint, of the conscience of the great convert of Jesus Christ, Paul of Tarsus. And I pray that the Lord may hear me and give me the strength to speak, according to the highest truth in me, without judging myself or, still less, others, about the tragic events in the history of the Jews of Rome at the time of the German invasion.

14. History of the Jews of Rome, 1943–1944

"Where Christ is, there is Life." These words of Saint Ambrose were a starting point for me in understanding the interior reality of Christianity's birth, growth, and driving force. The *Follow Me* was an invitation to follow the Master completely. The patriarchs walked before God; Christ's followers follow Christ, in Christ; and this opened to me the way to understand the mystery of the Mystical Body of Christ. The follower becomes a living and active cell in the Mystical Body, the Church of Christ. It is a *communion*, a bond that transcends the relation of blood and nation. Conversion is therefore thought of as baptism, rebirth, a second birth in the person, life, works—and above all in the death —of Christ. All things were new and interesting; not the least interesting was the conception of the Beyond, not as a great academy where the masters study the Law under the presidency of the Lord, and where Moses, hearing how he is quoted, does not recognize his text. The life of the Beyond is joy in Christ; it is the continuation of the spiritual symposium begun on earth, in the midst of sufferings, sacrifices, and martyrdom. In heaven, the communion with Christ becomes pure joy. We suffer, then we rejoice; we rise in Christ to live with Christ.

Communion with Christ is at the same time communion with Christ's followers. The followers of Christ—pastors, virgins, and the faithful—follow Christ on earth, and after death, they follow Him to the heavenly banquet. We work and labor with Christ, and we sit at the banquet table with Christ. It is an active participation in heaven and on earth for all who have done God's will on earth as it is done in heaven. The "Son of Man" appeared to the prophet Ezekiel under the likeness of "the Man Adam"—"Ben Adam"; *the Son of Man* is the highest expression of God in humanity. Man walks before God, takes refuge near God, hides under God's wings; he finds salvation in God; near God he sees God through Christ.

Christ is the Way of God, the Word of God, the Truth of God; Christ is the Way that leads man to God.

If such was indeed the being, the will, the work, and the teaching of Christ, was it not to be expected that He should proclaim Himself one with God? Is not Christ fully subject to the Father? Does He not say that these things are known only by the Father? Jesus and His disciples are called to prepare the Kingdom of heaven. Was not the Kingdom of God the highest desire of the most sublime genius of Israel? The Kingdom of God was to begin on earth, wrought not by the sword, nor with warlike valor, but in the Spirit of the Lord.

So I thought, and my thoughts were ever more deep and decisive during the horrors of the war and the cruel persecutions of the innocent—and first of all of the Chosen People, that people to whom I was bound with all the fibers of my heart.

It happened that a copy of a popular edition of the *Didache* (Doctrine of the Twelve Apostles) came into my hands. This is a book of moral and ritual teaching on the Eucharist, written toward the end of the first and the beginning of the second centuries after Christ. The thesis maintaining that the book first appeared in Egypt is not convincing; neither do I believe in a possible Syrian origin. The *Didache* impresses me as a small book of Jewish-Christian origin, written in the environs of Palestine. It fascinated me, for its character is profoundly Hebrew, although it is Greek in form. In it, Hebraism and Christianity are fused into a harmonious whole.

The thanksgiving for the Eucharist recalls the style of the Hebrew blessings of the table. In the Hebrew liturgy, a prayer is said for the reunion of the dispersed of Israel in their ancient fatherland. In the *Didache*, the desire is expressed for the gathering of the Church into the Kingdom of Christ, and this finds an echo in the words of Saint Paul (1 Cor 10:17): "For we, being many, are one bread, one body: all that partake of one bread."

It is my opinion that the *Didache* represents the Hebrew ritual of the Eucharist, as it was observed at the end of the first century on Palestinian soil. I read the *Didache* again in the Greek text, and it became most dear to me and gave me occasion for making a few more marginal notes. For instance, in the ninth chapter, at the beginning, we read: "As to the Eucharist, give thanks over the chalice in this way: We give Thee thanks; then over the broken bread: We give Thee thanks." Why first the chalice, then the broken bread?

The commentator, after stressing the fact that this refers to the Eucharistic species, goes on to say that the inverted order could not have such importance as to prevent this interpretation: namely, that here the Eucharist is referred to; besides, there is a significant warning given in the two brief prayers which follow: "No one ought to eat or drink of Your Eucharist who is not baptized in the name of the Lord." Hence this is surely said of the Eucharist.

Well and good, but this does not explain the inversion of the ritual order; indeed the warning mentions *first* the eating, then the drinking. The warning proves that the custom initiated by Jesus and always followed by the Church was, in fact, first the bread and then the wine, and not vice versa. So we must conclude (such is my opinion) that the author of the ritual followed in his mind the Sabbatic Festival, the *Hebrew* Banquet, in which indeed the order is first the wine, then the broken bread.

For years I remained chained, so to speak, to the apostolic doctrine on the Eucharist. I would steal a bit of time for myself now and then, even if I felt crushed by the weight of work, to return to the *Didache* and to the chapter on the Eucharist.

The Eucharist is the expression of the *unification* of the children of the Church dispersed, according to one version, "like the grains on the stems of many ears"; according to another version, "like the flour scattered on the table around which is now celebrated the Eucharist". The mixing has *unified* the flour for the Eucharist; the Eucharist unifies all those who, being baptized, partake of it.

If two or three or more virgins are present, they must also give thanks over the bread. The catechumens are excluded till they come to spiritual maturity. Also excluded are women whose moral and religious conduct is reprehensible. Absolute *purity* is the reason why to virgins, rather than to mothers of families, is reserved the giving of thanks. The virgins mixed the bread. The concept of purity in the *Didache* is remarkable. It is not like the sacerdotal Levitic purity but is rather a moral purity. "On the dominical day [Sunday] of the Lord, meet together, break the bread, give thanks, after having confessed your sins, so that your sacrifice may be pure."

One is aware of the teaching of Jesus Christ in the *Didache* (xiv, 2): "Whosoever has had a contention with his companion should not come to the gathering until he is reconciled, lest your offering be profaned." Why do we not think of the leaven fermenting in hearts, of bitterness against one's neighbor?

How elevating and apt the application of Malachi's text to the Eucharist: "The word of the Lord: In every place [and time] there is offered to my name a clean oblation . . . for I am a great king and my love is wonderful among the Gentiles." What mystery in the final prayer: "Let grace come; and this world pass away." The partakers of Holy Communion see with the eyes of the spirit the rising of another world—a new world.

The Hebrew Paschal Supper has, in Aramaic, at the beginning, an invitation: "Whosoever is hungry, let him come and eat. Around the table are those who have provided for their comfort—and the others? Let them come near." In the *Didache*, thought is given to those who have provided good things for their soul—and the others? "If anyone is holy, let him approach. If anyone is not so" (what delicacy of expression, so often encountered in the Bible), "let him repent."

Many times the Redeemer appeared to His disciples during meals. With what nostalgia Israel awaits, during the Paschal Supper, the appearance of the prophet Elijah, of Elijah who was taken up toward heaven—the prophet who will appear before the day of the Lord arrives.

At the end of the sacred Eucharistic banquet, the expectation of Jesus is most lively; Jesus is in all hearts. One can hear from a distance His gentle step—how beautiful upon the mountains, the steps of Him who brings good tidings to Zion—saying to Zion: "Behold your God!" Nostalgia for God is resplendent and burning like a sacred flame; from the heart breaks out, high and urgent, the Aramaic cry: *Maranatha!* Come, Lord! Come, Lord!

I was deep in thought. I lived again in those distant times, in that distant land, the sanctity of the Expectation; an expectation that was so keen in the years of my childhood now far away: *Maran-atha!* Come, Lord!

Of a sudden I heard the rumble of cannons above all other sounds—the Germans were approaching Rome.

Taine says that sickness is the natural state of man, and that perfect health is an exception realized in particularly favorable circumstances. Living is, of itself, a continual oscillation between well-being and sickness, between life and death. Someone has remarked lately that, in the literature of the people of the valley of Mesopotamia, the word "death" (*mêtu*) can sometimes mean "to be in danger of death, to be unfortunate"; whereas the word meaning "to live" (*balâtu*), corresponding to the Hebrew *palat*, means "to save oneself, to escape". To live means to escape sickness and death.

Of this biological process, an analogy is found in community life. Man, pushed by the necessities of life, cooperates with his neighbor, but soon cooperation degenerates into a scheme for enslaving the collaborators. This temptation to take advantage of the co-worker is keenest in a person of conscious superiority, who readily feels contempt for apparent weakness in one he regards as an inferior, even though this "inferior" has succeeded in keeping pace with the accomplishments of his associates. Thereupon the collaborator or neighbor of yesterday is judged today to be a parasite, to be attacked by the machine of war if it be a people or a state, to be suppressed by the weapons of society if it be a small, undefended minority.

On the eve of the invasion of Rome by the Germans, the Jews found themselves facing two undeniable facts: they were Italians like the others, and they were Jews unlike the others. What were they to expect from the coming together of the S.S., the worst elements of the Germans, with the worst elements of the National Fascist Party? I have always been opposed to generalizations, e.g., the nobility, the plebeians, a certain nation, a certain religion, or a certain family, being, as I am, an exponent of the autonomy of the human person. Were I desirous of expressing my apprehensions in the shape of a problem in mathematics, I should have done it this way: P.N.F. + S.S. = X. X, a terrible unknown, quantitatively; a disastrous kind; quantitatively not yet determined; certainly portending great woes.

The effects of the incomprehension with which I met on the part of both the President of the Union of the Italian Israelite Communities and the President of the Israelite Community of Rome were so terrible, so tragic, but I refuse to believe that there was any lack of good will. No, I repeat, it was not ill-will; but when one has passed through certain schools and disciplines, one acquires a mentality conformable to that school. For my part, in Trieste, I had had long conversations with Dr. Armand Kaminka of Vienna, with Professor Torczyer of the University of Jerusalem, expelled from Berlin, and with hundreds of fugitives from the most varied regions, from the most different countries under the yoke and influence of Nazism. In Trieste also I had had the opportunity of reading all kinds of documents that placed before my eyes the whole reality of the terrifying situation. In addition to this, in Rome, I learned through a high Catholic ecclesiastic who had long been a friend of our family and was acquainted with a Catholic employee of the German embassy that we might expect persecution. During the course of the German occupation, I was kept informed through this source of the German plans with regard to the Jews as they developed. Since this information was obtained and transmitted to me only out of Christian charity and at enormous risk to my informants, I was never at liberty to reveal their identities to the men whom I had to persuade of the imminent danger to the Jewish population.

With regard to the probability of persecution in Rome, there was this to be said: the influence of the Vatican was great, and open persecution was certain to produce a great outcry from the Pope. The number of Jews was small, and the Germans had little to gain from their elimination. It was known that the German army was opposed to persecution on political grounds. But reason had little hold on the S.S., and the question was whether or not they could be restrained. My whole experience argued against the possibility of their being restrained more than temporarily. The contrary judgment of the two Presidents was due, I think, simply to their lack of this experience.

I should like to say here that the people of Rome loathed the Nazis and had intense pity for the Jews. They would willingly have assisted in the evacuation of the Jewish population into remote villages, where they would have been concealed and protected by Christian families. Christian families in the heart of Rome would have accepted Jews. There was money in the treasury for the support of destitute refugees thus hidden. The Holy Father sent by hand a letter to the bishops instructing them to lift the enclosure from convents and monasteries, so that they could become refuges for the Jews. I know of one convent where the sisters slept in the basement, giving up their beds to Jewish refugees. In face of this charity, the fate of so many of the persecuted is especially tragic.

But to return to the evening before the Germans entered Rome: I called the President of the Union (of the Italian Israelite Communities) by phone from the usher's office at the temple. I felt that, as ex-Prefect and ex-Vice Head of the Fascist police, he would understand. I said: "They are about to enter. Tomorrow they will be here. Let us meet with the President of the Community [of Rome]. Do invite him"— I knew with whom I was dealing—"to be at your office tomorrow at seven. I shall tell you what I think must be done to protect the Israelite population. If you follow me, I will take upon myself the greater part of the responsibility for the transformation and the adaptation. If only you agree and act at once."

"Ha, ha, ha!" He laughed, and his laughter was so loud that it was heard by Mrs. Gemma, an usher in the temple, who was holding a candle near me. (It was the only light we could use, as electric lights had been forbidden.)

"Ha, ha, ha! How can a mind as clear as yours think of interrupting the regular functioning of offices and the regular conduct of Hebrew life? As recently as yesterday, I went to the Minister and received quite reassuring information. Do not worry."

"But you see—"

"No, I repeat that you can keep quite calm. And moreover, you must communicate absolute confidence to the people. Don't worry, and have a good night. Good night."

I hung up the receiver, and turning to the brave Mrs. Gemma, I said, "Remember, in Rome there will be a bath of blood. Who knows how many Jews will pay with their life?"

I returned home. The night was not as good as the gentleman had wished me. There was a continuous rumbling of cannons and the wail of sirens. The canteen used as refuge from bombings was cold, damp, and dusty.

On the morrow, I waited for four hours for the President of the Community to get into touch with me. He did not even telephone. The offices were deserted. The guns sounded nearer and nearer; the sirens were heard now and then. From time to time, we went to the refuge; we came up and then went down again. I did not want to go up and down those stairs at all. I was praying in my heart: We are willing to fall into the hands of the Lord, because His mercy is great. Preserve us from falling into the hands of men!

It was afternoon. I went to visit the Regional Commissioner of Police. He was a fine, honest man, an anti-Fascist. "What must I do?" I asked him.

As one politically heterodox, he was listening to the London radio. He said, "If I have understood right, one hour after entering Prague, they killed the Chief Rabbi of that city. In my opinion, you ought to leave your house for three or four days, until you see what system they will adopt here. After that, you will be able to judge for yourself. At the moment, I have nothing more to say. We functionaries, as you see, have no uniform; we have received orders to wear civilian clothes. We are waiting. We ourselves do not know which way to turn."

I returned home. I had hardly shut the door when from the nearby streets I heard shrieks of fright and anguish: "The Germans! The Germans!"

My daughter Miriam, pale and troubled, ran to the street and returned. "Away at once!" she said. "Here we are at the entrance of the Ghetto; everyone is fleeing." She started to pack some linen. "I have put out the fire", she said. "Let us leave everything and go."

"But", I said, "I would like to take with me—"

"You will take nothing, Father; we must survive. Here we shall die!"

We walked under the hissing of bullets. Where to? I did not know. My daughter walked behind her ailing mother. I followed. An elderly Italian soldier warned me to keep close to the wall. "Where are you going?" I asked him. "How do things look?"

"Nothing more to do", he answered. "I shall go home and put on civilian clothes, and tomorrow I shall look for work. My wife and children are hungry." When we reached the corner of the street, I gave him a few cigarettes and a small gift for the children. We shook hands and parted.

We walked on. Finally, my dear wife could go no farther. It was raining, and we were too lightly clad for the weather. We were hungry, but there was no time to notice hunger and fatigue. There were no means of transportation to be found—not a taxi anywhere. We were near the Palace of Justice. I looked up at the building and said to myself, as I usually do in such moments: Justice? Where is justice?

Is it just, I thought, all that is going on? Should not justice be a *reasonable* thing? Would it not have been just and reasonable to meet this morning at seven to coordinate our ideas and plans? Why are the people left in ignorance, without directions? I had, and still have, a clear plan, based on a realistic view of things. My ideas could be modified and completed—but why are they rejected outright?

We entered the apartment of the kind Fiorentino family, two old people and their son. We were some distance from the place destined to be the center of the upheaval. We were received with great goodness. All were sad. Their kindness was a great comfort. My wife and daughter were invited to spend the night there.

The young doorkeeper was intelligent and friendly. After dusk I started down the dark streets, seeking a refuge for myself. I said to my dear ones before leaving that I was certain to find someplace. I dragged myself to the house of an "Aryan" friend, a person of means and influence, with whom I had done scientific research. He had a beautiful living room with a divan that no one used at night. I asked, "Let me spend the night here, I beg of you!"

"It is impossible! I'll give you a note to . . ."

"Thank you, that's fine."

I walked the unfamiliar streets in the thick darkness, and finally I arrived. A man from whom I asked directions looked at me with compassion. "Come with me", he said; "it is very difficult for one who is not familiar with these narrow streets." I realized that he was trying to comfort me. I rang the bell, trusting in the magic power of the note. But I soon realized that a telephone call had preceded me.

"You know . . . for us."

"I understand. See", I said, "a chair is enough for me even in the dark corridor. I have some cigarettes with me, and everything else I need." But nothing could be done. He saw my consternation and explained how he had been treated with great cordiality by this one and by that one. What was I to do, seeing that it was forbidden to go about at night without a special permit? I will go to my own house, I said to myself. But how ridiculous! said a voice within me. Home? You have no home. You are a wandering dog. If that phrase offends you, I shall say you are a wandering Jew. What ugly things you are saying, I said to myself.

Finally I arrived. I put the key in the door, and it did not work as easily as usual. I stood there alone.

A night guard at the corner of the street approached me in the dark. "Give me the key a moment, Professor." Strange, I thought. I, Professor? Is it possible?

"The Lord help you, Professor!"

"And you, also; may He help us all!"

I was dripping with sweat. I washed and changed my clothes, all in the dark. I stretched out on my bed. I prayed.

Then . . . Will there be the sudden stroke of a bell? A knock on the door? I am on the list of the Nazi Party. I am a Jew; I have no city. I am the Chief Rabbi of the Roman Community. What an array of choice qualities in one individual!

I lay motionless with eyes wide open and listened . . . listened to the silence, and over me descended a deep, black silence.

The learning process is a thing that can be accomplished exclusively by the intellect without any modification of the mentality as a whole—for example, a child learning that six times six makes thirty-six. But there is another kind of learning that involves the whole personality. An old oculist, Dr. Spierer, told me once that although he was not a believer, he felt the Spirit of God near him when he wondered at the wisdom revealed in the anatomy of the eye. The truth is that the knowledge we derive from experience depends much on what we bring to the learning process. I, for example, am not only moved by reading the Psalms; sometimes the analysis of an isolated word in one of the Semitic languages also has power to stir me. Men can communicate with each other by means of the intellect, and especially by having recourse to the heart.

In view of this subjective element, I can understand how it is that a man endowed with much pride, *must* tend to attribute to his own plan of action such importance as not to *be able* to accept the plan of another, or submit his own to a critical examination. In the "I think", "I will", "I" is placed before the function of thinking and willing without an object, or the just evaluation of the object. The preponderance of the "I" in judging involves a priori the predicates "well" and "useful for others and self." Such a man does not fully evaluate other peoples' opinions; an opinion different from his cannot be a good opinion, and still less can it be the best. Truth has *already* spoken.

This state of things is aggravated in certain men of law, who for years, with all the means at their disposal, have aimed at demonstrating that only *their* opinion is *just*. Every defendant or accuser must prove his own thesis to be the just one, and if the evidence is not certain, he will have recourse to pointing out some defect of form to overthrow the other's thesis. Thus it happens that the issue in question is inadvertently removed from the sphere of what is just, true, and useful, in this man's effort to prove his point well, i.e., successfully, with as much art as possible, though it may not be for his own good. So it often is, alas!

In the period of the occupation of Rome by the military forces and the terrifying German S.S., there was a sharp difference of opinion between the two men who were the chief representatives of Italian Hebraism. The President of the Community of Rome held to autonomy, to the independence of his local community from the central power (the Union of Italian Israelite Communities). So far as I was concerned, my opinion had little weight, for the Rabbi, despite the important-sounding title he bears—"Most Excellent"—is but a salaried employee. He may think, he may propose, and no more. Under the best of circumstances, the employee proposes, but—the President disposes.

I was convinced that we should busy ourselves in the interests of the Israelite population, which was now at the mercy of the Germans. I had concrete ideas on the subject, but the two Presidents were convinced that nothing ought to be done. I knew both men well, and I knew that if I had the President of the Roman Community on my side, I could sway the President of the Union, who was a man of years and prudence.

On the morning after that memorable night, my family and I were able to take over, for a few days, an apartment left vacant by some Jews who, like many others, had fled. We were warned that if the bell at the entrance, or the telephone, should ring, we were not to answer; we were to play dead. Everyone I could get to, I counseled to leave Rome, or to seek refuge in a convent. And I begged them to notify their relatives and friends to do the same. The present calm, I felt, could not last long. My daughter, together with the young lawyer Fiorentino, tried, so far as they could, to give the alarm in my name to whomever they met, always asking them to pass the word on.

After three days, I came out, so to speak, from the belly of the whale and went to the office. The employees were in terror and confusion. Jews were standing about in groups in front of the temple. "And you, what are you doing here?" I asked. "Disperse and go as far away as you can." (At other times, as I have said, my daughter did this work. They thanked her and obeyed, at least for the moment.)

In the offices there was no one except the employees. I waited a long time; finally the President (of the Community) came. He was sober and worried. We began to talk— or rather, I began to talk. He was taciturn, but fortunately he listened. In this word *fortunately* there is no irony. I thanked God for that in my heart, for I said: If the Lord assists me, I shall succeed.

"Listen, Mr. President", I said, "give orders that the temple and all the oratories be closed. Send all the employees home and close the offices. Let the secretary, lawyer P. (a man of years and to be trusted), draw one million lire, or even two, from the bank; and give all the employees three months' advance pay. All this will give a little alarm to these thousands of people who are going about the streets of the

Ghetto ignorant of the danger. Give to a committee of three whom you trust a large sum of money to subsidize the exodus of the poorest. You will see that the first ten families will be a good example to the others. Solemn funerals must be handed over to Aryans of the city. The prayers can be said at home; the same for other functions. Let everyone pray where he is; after all, God is everywhere. All this is absolutely necessary, especially now in the fall, when there are so many great solemnities. We have thousands of Roman Jews and thousands from other cities who have taken refuge here. The Germans can surround the temple and the oratories with their cannons and guns exactly at the hour when those places are jammed with people." I stopped and did not say any more. I thought it better to wait.

He was silent. Then he rang a little bell, and in came the Secretary. We have brought it off, I thought. Can it be?

"Is Miss S. P. in the office?"

"No, she is afraid."

"Notify her that she is fired."

"Yes, sir", replied the Secretary, and went out.

"We are alone again", he said to me. "You should be giving courage instead of spreading discouragement. I have received assurances—. As to your proposals, I shall keep the Major Temple and all the oratories *open*."

The answer was very clear, and it was quite understandable on the part of a magistrate who had been a brave officer of the First World War. Then too, the statute of the Community spoke clearly: In *nonreligious* questions, the President together with his Council shall decide—and the Council was most obedient. Men in general do not readily assume responsibilities; they do not know what should be done and do not like to think. Anyone who knows how to command is thought sure to be right, and "authoritative" becomes synonymous with "authorized". The President saw things his way; he was convinced that he was doing right. There had been a time when he would have followed my advice, but the wind had changed. Neither this man nor those who shared the responsibility for the events of the near future ever imagined that while they followed their chosen line of conduct a disaster was being prepared.

I felt that the ground was mined under our feet. I bade him good-day and went out, determined to return again. As I went down the stairs to go home, I was followed by two men. One, in civilian clothes, said casually to the other, *"Dass ist der mann!"* ("That is the man!"). They were the Gestapo. They must not have been well informed, because at the usher's office, they had asked for Rabbi *Prato*, who was then in Palestine. You may well understand that I took an opposite direction to the one I ought to have followed, entering into a maze of narrow, unfrequented streets. They did not follow me there, because decisions were not yet mature. In fact, two days later, the informants of whom I have spoken sent word to me through my daughter that the Wehrmacht did not want to stage a persecution in Rome under the eyes of the Vatican, and that the S.S. were still under control. I returned home and asked myself: What ought I to do next?

I let a day go by so as to avoid being tracked, and the day following I went to the President of the Union. This man of years, this ex-political functionary, listened to me graciously. "I guarantee safety for you and for your wife also", he said.

"Thank you, Your Excellency", I answered. Again I wished we had been three to discuss the matter. *"We must* take some measures to protect the population. As for our person, after having done what is our duty toward those entrusted to us, each one will do what he thinks best for himself. *We must* disperse the people. The Jews must not move en masse, lest they be easy targets for flying projectiles. Single men may be killed, of course, but we shall have avoided a general slaughter."

He answered, "I do not share your fears in the least."

And *here* is the tragic point of the situation. Fear, courage, love, and sorrow are emotions that cannot be communicated in their reality. Both the Presidents had had categorical assurances from high personages in whom they had unshakable confidence, and in the face of such information, precautionary measures seemed like the product of childish fears. Children are afraid of the dark, and we try to convince them that there is no *reason* to be afraid.

Reason and logic were on their side. Had not the "powerful" Italian-constituted Authorities given explicit assurances? Is it not true that in Rome not a single Hebrew has been hurt?

"But, pardon me, Your Excellency; even granting that my preoccupations are groundless, and they *are not*, what do you lose by listening to me? Invite the other President."

"If you both wish to come", he added, "let me know, and I will await you with pleasure." There was little cause for rejoicing!

Friday I went to a meeting of the Council of Administration of the Israelite Hospital. There I met a great benefactress of the hospital and other such organizations, Miss Cavalieri, the President of the Charity Commission, Mr. James Di Segni, and others. Miss Cavalieri, an elderly woman, said, "But you, Professor, why are you roaming around here? It is dangerous not only for you but for us also. If they arrest you, it is more probable that they will think of us too. You are too daring! Go into hiding, I beg of you!"

And Mr. Di Segni said, "Yesterday, when I was passing through Piazza Pasquale Paoli with my son, two German soldiers were busy carrying away leather from a store. They commanded us to load the material onto the truck. We had to obey. They pressed several others into service too; one of them, unfortunately, was a priest. After an hour, I tried to tell them by pointing to my heart that I was suffering and could not continue the work. I know no German. One of the Germans went out, got hold of another passer-by and showed me the door. I had much difficulty in freeing my son. I was afraid that they would ask if we were Jews."

Already the situation was getting worse, and I shared Miss Cavalieri's opinion. "What shall I say, my friends?" I replied. "I know through information received and from experience that we can expect no easy time of it. If I am still wandering about, it is only for a few days; after that, either I shall succeed in saving myself or else they will kill me—or, more probably, deport me and kill me somewhere else. In any case, I can't wander for long. I beg you to help me to influence the President. I'm afraid that he is far too confident regarding the lot of the Jewish population."

No one answered me. Then I said to myself that I might as well return to the President of the Community, so I did.

"What is the news in your office?" he said.

"It is deserted", I said. I did not dare to say that not even the doorkeeper had reported. (Poor man, he was taken later, deported, and killed. Only a few weeks after the conversation at the hospital, Miss Cavalieri was deported and killed.) I continued, "Pardon my insistence, but what harm would be done if the two of us went now and paid a visit to His Excellency? Just for an exchange of ideas in view of an eventual decision."

"If precautions are to be taken—and there is no need for

them—I ought to take them with my Council. For the moment nothing is to be decided. You should buy a pennysworth of courage at the drugstore."

I did not answer that, but went on. "See, *I* could leave the cards with the addresses of our contributors up to date. Two or three employees could transcribe the addresses into a book that could be deposited quietly with a trustworthy Aryan notary. I know that the directors of the High Roman Israelite School have destroyed their files."

This time it was the President who did not answer. I felt it to be a silence of death.

A man in certain situations does not know how to escape from himself. He becomes his own prisoner. This is the truth that I tell you in Christ. I *understand* the incomprehension of others, and I do not judge. These two men did not know the Germans, especially when they are drunk with an ideal, and *this is the reason why* they did not understand me, but declared me "unqualified". There were forces, local and nonlocal, operating to vitiate the thinking of these two deserving and well-intentioned men. No one is stronger than himself. Confidence in me had been shaken. It had been the work of others, far away in space but near in spirit with all their interests.

The whole situation can be summed up in these terms. To me it was given to see without being able to act; to others the power to act without the gift to see, to provide.

I felt that the refusal to destroy the list of addresses of contributors was a very serious thing. Two more lists were in existence: one at the Ministry of Interior and the other in the City Hall, but these addresses were not up-to-date or complete, and perhaps some employee might destroy them. At the Office of Civilian Affairs, partisans and other zealous employees were forever fabricating documents with imaginary data and names to be used by Hebrews. Not even King Solomon could have penetrated to the identity of those who carried them. Best of all, this took place under the vigilant eyes of the Germans. But the file of the Community was not like those "documents".

Alas for files of the Community! There is a legend about them that is not historical; but they had a true history, and it was tragic.

This is the story. The head usher at that time, Mr. Romeo Bondi, said to me, "I was behind you when you made the request to destroy the files. The other gentleman did not answer. Instead, he said to you: 'If the Duce proclaims himself Head of the State, we will have to remove the portrait of the King.' You remained silent at this observation."

This same Bondi knows exactly what happened to the files during the German occupation. It was he who was sent, by order of the President, to surrender the files on the demand of the political authorities of "liberated" Italy.

At this time Bondi drew out of his pocket a small package of cards, several of which were stained with mud. The one on duty at the temple, a certain S., spread the report that the files had been deposited in the cellars of the temple. That is not true. That is the legend. And if they had been deposited there—and, I repeat, it is not true that they were—it would have been a mistake; they should have been destroyed.

Frederick, the porter of the house in which I lived, was pleasant and friendly. What could be more natural than if my daughter, accompanied by Dr. Fiorentino, should pay him a visit? Under such circumstances one can talk about everything—the health of this one and that one, the price of wine. Toward the end of the visit Frederick remarked in a casual way and with a knowing smile that German "Jews", very well-dressed and well-shaven, were continually coming to the door asking for the Professor's new address, because, they said, "we need his counsel"! What an honor; to be a counselor of the Gestapo is no small thing!

One day Mr. Pierantoni was passing the Opera House. (He was a pensioned employee of the Ministry, a man who had seen the world—well-educated, very intelligent, familiar with the interior of Italian prisons and an empty wallet. Every so often he was sent to breathe the temperate air of some jail! There was some justice in this, since he was a bitter anti-Fascist. His son, Dr. Luigi, an officer of the Red Cross, surpassed his father in anti-Nazism. He was denounced, and later on was shot in the Fosse Ardeatine.) Mr. Pierantoni was approached by an agent of the Gestapo, who, with a polite bow, asked, in atrocious Italian, where the great Rabbi of Rome *lived now.*

Mr. Pierantoni quickly sought refuge in self-depreciation (in Florence we would say, "He became as tall as two pennysworth of cheese") and proceeded to identify himself. "I not Rome, I Viterbo. I sell potatoes to eat." (Clearness of exposition is a virtue.) "I know only potato shops."

The agent, on hearing all this said, "You're welcome", by which he meant, "Excuse me."

It is not for nothing that Pierantoni's hair is white, and not for nothing was he Head of the Cabinet of the Governor in Somalia. At the "You're welcome" of the German, this fellow countryman of Macchiavelli responded with a double "You're welcome, you're welcome." The agent now walked toward the Corso, and Pierantoni followed him. He observed that the good man entered one store after another, made a deep bow, asked a question, but never bought a thing.

Mr. Pierantoni then got in touch with his son; his son

notified Miss Mariu, who was then carrying on a bold anti-Nazi campaign. As women cannot be silent, Mariu got into conversation with her friend, Miss Miriam Zolli, who must be tested. She said to her: "This evening at eight o'clock, an auto will stop before the house where your parents are. They have been found out. They must get into the auto with Fiorentino. The chauffeur is one of our own. At a certain point, Fiorentino will leave the car with your mother and will accompany her to a low-class, and therefore safer, boarding-house. It is, of course, right opposite the German headquarters." (What a terrifying girl dear Mariu is!) "Your father will ride on to the Square of Porta Pia and have a cup of coffee at the bar on the corner. Later a young woman will arrive on a bicycle—me. She will sit down and start reading a novel. Your father will leave the bar. I shall follow. I shall walk off, and he will follow. Clear?"

Then came the visits! Miriam, Fiorentino, and the lawyer Ruggero Di Segni, Councillor of the Community, and another young man—all friends. I tried to oppose the plan, but to what purpose? My daughter became ferocious (that is the right word). "I could not survive the capture of you and mother. I would kill myself", she said.

Poor creature, she was pale, and trembling all over. "They have been at Mariu's house asking about you", she said. "I shall place you in safety and then go in search of a refuge in some forgotten village of the Abruzzi. It will not be easy, but at least I shall know that you are both safe. Now give me a kiss and show that you are a good, God-fearing father. Good fathers always obey their daughters." She wiped away her tears. "Mother, you prepare the luggage." What irony! A briefcase with a few old clothes.

Mariu takes me from street to street, through ways unknown to me. Passing by, she knocks at the window of a house. Who knows why? And still we walk. The whole thing is so very romantic. We stand before a green meadow. See who is here! Casually, Dr. Luigi Pierantoni comes up! Now we are three. They talk to each other, in good Italian, of other cases, people to be saved. I had not understood it at the time, but suddenly it dawned on me. The knock at the window had meant: Go to the appointment by another route; I have him with me.

There is a brief good-bye. Miss Mariu slips swiftly away. We are now two, and we walk in silence through deserted streets. The darkness deepens, and it is welcome to the good doctor. "It is here, follow me", he says.

In about two minutes, the door opens: behold the potato merchant from Viterbo! "This little room belongs to my other son, who is under Badoglio's command", he explains. "Luigi will go home now. Let us have supper. We shall be alone. Cigarettes are a great boon in these times, aren't they?"

At half-past eleven, we listen to the radio from Moscow —illegal, of course. "Let us hear how many defeats the Germans have had", he says. "Down with the German invaders!"

By this time the German police were going out every night in search of Jews. Owing to the loss of our records, the fact that no count could be made of the numbers of Jews who had come to Rome from other places and were caught, and the secrecy with which much of the S.S.'s program was conducted, no reliable statistics are available as to the number of Jews who perished during the occupation of the city. Thousands were deported and killed, hundreds died in Roman prisons. We were helpless, never knowing where disaster would strike next. My nights were semi-vigils. Lord, I prayed, let me die with the others when and how you wish, but not as the Germans wish! Have mercy on all men, upon all your children!

For nine months, the Wehrmacht continued to defend itself from its enemies, while keeping Rome in its grasp, but the Hebrews could not defend themselves against the S.S. Early in the occupation, before the S.S. had received any authorization to attack the Jews, one of their commanders, on his own authority, began the assault upon the treasury of the Community with the demand: *Fifty kilograms of gold within twenty-four hours; otherwise, three hundred hostages will be taken.*

A plenary session of the Council was called. I sent word that my presence would not be in the least helpful, since the discussion would be exclusively of financial matters. If I could do something—anything at all—they could count on me. I would do it regardless of danger. Meanwhile I sent my gold chain and five thousand lire. I provided my daughter with the opportunity of going in a car, for greater security and to save time, to collect gold rings without stones. She did so, and succeeded in a remarkable manner, and was thanked.

At seven next morning Dr. Pierantoni came to my room. The Community had succeeded in gathering together only around thirty-five kilograms of gold. Would I, he asked, go to the Vatican and try to obtain a loan of fifteen kilograms of gold?

"Right away", I replied.

Dr. Fiorentino arrived with a car.

"I am dressed like a beggar", I remarked. "We shall go in by one of the back doors", he replied. "The Vatican is always guarded by the Gestapo. A friendly person will be waiting for you, and so that you can avoid showing personal documents stamped 'Hebrew Race', you will be presented as an engineer, called to examine some walls that are being constructed."

"The art of examining walls has always interested me", I answered.

The builders greeted me; I let them talk; I gave my approval to the construction problem presented to me. Very comic! Then we walked and walked till we came to the office of the Head of the Treasury, then to that of the Secretary of State.

The Vatican had already spent millions in aiding fugitive Jews to reach safety. I said, "The New Testament does not abandon the Old. Please help me. As for repayment, I myself shall stand as surety, and since I am poor, the Hebrews of the whole world will contribute to pay the debt."

Both the Treasurer and the Monsignori were moved. The Treasurer disappeared, and after a few minutes returned. He had gone to the Holy Father. "Come back shortly before one o'clock. The offices will be deserted, but two or three employees will be here waiting for you and will give you the package. You may leave a receipt in the form of a simple note. There will be no difficulty."

"Please give my thanks to His Holiness", I said. I went back to the house of Fiorentino.

I wrote a letter to the President of the Community and told him everything, adding that in case hostages were demanded, I should want to head the list as a volunteer. I had Fiorentino read the letter. He put it in the envelope I had prepared and took it by car to my daughter, who delivered it personally into the hands of the President.

This narrative could now be considered complete—and, in fact, need not have been included in this book—if it were not for the following events: After the liberation, the President of the Israelite Community of Rome denied having received my letter concerning the gold and my offer to be a voluntary hostage, saying that I had not offered my co-operation; that I had stopped coming to the office during the time of the occupation; that I had never proposed any precautions for the protection of the Israelite population of Rome.

In view of these charges, I feel, therefore, that it is my duty to publish a few documents that are in my possession and that have passed the Tribunal of Rome. They are presented as an appendix to this book. I also include there the letter of the President in which he made the assertions referred to above, and a copy of the session of the Board, which, on the basis of these charges, dismissed me from the office of Chief Rabbi of the Community of Rome, in April 1944. Among these documents will be found one (Document *H*) from Professor Elena Sonnino-Finzi, daughter of the lamented Chief Rabbi of Genoa, of whose death I shall now give a brief account.

My program of rescue included also the proposal of a trip to be made by the usher of the temple, Mrs. Gemma Contardi. She, provided with regular papers, was to visit the larger communities to notify them by word of mouth of the impending danger and to cause the same advice to reach minor centers, also by word of mouth. But this action was prevented, and this is what happened in the other cities:

Deported and put to death were the Chief Rabbi of Modena, Dr. Rodolphe Levi; the Chief Rabbi of Bologna, Albert Orvieto; and the Chief Rabbi of Genoa, Dr. Richard Pacifici.

This last, out of excessive zeal, stayed in his office at a time when I had concealed myself, though I remained at the disposition of the Community for any work of real value, and not purely formal. Dr. Pacifici had a visit from the persecutors. They beat him and forced him to call the Jewish families by telephone and bid them come to him, since he "had a secure refuge for them". People came in numbers. The Germans loaded them on trucks. The number of the victims would have been greater had not a few doorkeepers from the nearby houses (Aryans), in a casual way gone through the streets warning the Hebrew men, women, and children to flee.

Soon after that a foreign radio announced that poor Dr. Pacifici had been killed.

15. The Americans

The months immediately preceding the coming of the Americans were months of suffering. The small room in Mr. Pierantoni's house was like a refrigerator. In Rome, as everywhere, food was scarce. Mr. Pierantoni might have collected my salary, had not the President cut it off. Meanwhile, German officers and soldiers had broken into my house in search of documents of a political character. It was in vain, because I am by principle nonpolitical. In retaliation for their disappointment they left the doors open, and hoodlums went in and carried away everything; not a towel or a handkerchief was left.

My wife and I suffered much from hunger, cold, and anxiety for six months. The mental suffering was worst. I had not even a book with which to occupy my mind—an algebra manual and a dilapidated English grammar found in a corner had little interest for me.

Then there came a night of terrible suspense. The hospital of the Red Cross where the son of my host was serving was surrounded by armed Germans. Poor Luigi was put in jail. I set myself to burning printed messages having to do with the anti-Nazi underground and scoured the premises in search of weapons or explosives that might have been hidden by partisans of the Nazis so that they could be found by Nazi search parties and used as evidence against my host. This had happened in other cases.

In the morning, a young woman came to pay us a casual visit, a very, very "Aryan" girl—my eldest daughter, Dora, who with her husband and her little son had been

"Aryanized" (fictitiously) in the diocese of Milan by a pastor called Don Mario, perhaps at the suggestion of Cardinal Schuster.

"Come to us, Father, for a few days", she said.

"No", I answered, "you are safe; you are young; I am an old rag."

"I am going to repeat all this to Victor; then you will see", she threatened. She went off.

Within an hour she was back. She took my baggage, which consisted of my briefcase. "I shall carry this", she said. "We shall not know each other in the trolley. When I leave the car, you get off too and follow some way behind me. When I arrive at my house, I shall go in, but you walk up and down the street. Victor will presently join you. You must wait for the moment when the portress goes off duty to eat before you can come in."

Victor arrived. We kept moving, returning at intervals to a point from which we could see the house. Half an hour passed, an hour, another hour and fifteen minutes. Still no sign of my nephew Renatino, a most intelligent boy, who was to give us our cue. He was supposed to play around and watch the movements of the portress. On the window sill of my daughter's apartment hung a red carpet—another property in the stage setting.

I said to Victor, "It is evident that the portress' last meal was very substantial."

"Yes", he agreed. "Had I known, I would have given her some pills to stimulate her appetite." But a second later he said: 'There! Dora has taken in the red carpet. The coast is clear!" At the same moment Renatino came toward us in pursuit of his ball.

After two weeks, I decided that I must not stay any longer, but should return to Pierantoni. For I had perceived that

Victor and Dora were trembling for Renatino. "The will of God be done", they said. "Stay a few more days, and we will see."

One day soon after that my daughter returned from shopping and said, "You know, Father, I have met a friend of mine, a certain Emilia Falconieri, and she is coming here to visit us. When she comes you need not lock yourself up in the other room." (Habitually, when the doorbell rang, I hid, so as not to compromise the little "Aryan" family. My daughter was always anxious for her little son. Poor Dora! Today she seemed a little more at ease.)

The following day the bell rang. Who is it? Emilia! She comes up to me, places her hand on my shoulder, and says, "Listen, John" (It is the first time that she has ever seen me, and she calls me John!). "I have lost my father, and my husband, Gino, has lost his, so tomorrow you must come to us. You will be Papà Giovanni. You will be good to us, and love us, won't you?"

"Why not", I answer, "if you are good and obedient."

"Most obedient, Papà Giovanni", she assured me. Then we had a cup of coffee—a great luxury in those days—and there was more shaking of hands.

"We shall see you tomorrow", I said.

The day after I took on my new role. I have a small room, neat and shining, a book on the history of art. I am forbidden to go near the window on account of the neighbors. From time to time, Emilia comes to greet me. Sometimes she will be going out with a package.

"Where are you going?" I ask.

"I am carrying some food to Mother Emma: they have little to eat there."

Sometimes she returns with Mother Emma, and in the evening she accompanies her back to her home, not without the package for the next day. Gino comes home at night and places a small package on the table. "Here, Giovanni, for you—cigarettes."

But I was aware all these weeks that Miriam was suffering; my pennies were numbered. Still I was doing what was in my power, and salvation was near.

One day, late in the evening, we heard men singing. Gino dashed downstairs like a madman. The Americans had come!

Among many Americans we ought not to forget Colonel Poletti!

As the action of the President of the Community and his board, together with his attitude had "knocked me out", deposed me from the office of Chief Rabbi, and since I no longer made any attempt to defend myself, I could not and would not accept the invitation of General Johnson, sent to me from his office, to celebrate a *Te Deum*, inserting in the service a radio talk in English. I said I was sick. Because I had failed to accept, I received on June 30, 1944, the following letter from the Regional Commissioner, Colonel Charles Poletti:

Headquarters
Allied Military Government
Rome Region
APO 394   30th June 1944.

To the Chief Rabbi of the
Jewish Community of Rome,
Professor Israel Zolli,
V.S. Bartolomeo dei Vaccinari 19
Rome

Sir,

I have learned with deepest regret that you are passing through a crisis in your health. I wish to express my sincerest hope that as soon as you recover, you will resume your activity in full.

It is my desire that, during a time like the present, the direction of all affairs inherent to the rabbinical office, as well as the task of presiding over the solemn functions, should be entrusted to the expert and reliable hands of the religious leader himself.

It will be greatly appreciated if you will personally supervise preparations for the special Divine Service that has been the subject of a verbal communication. I have not yet had the pleasure of meeting you, but I expect to have this honor in the near future.

Sincerely yours,
Charles Poletti
Colonel U.S.A.
Regional Commissioner

Not long after this, the proposed meeting took place. Colonel Poletti began by saluting me courteously; then we passed on to speak of the General's invitation and of my illness, which was becoming more and more grave during the course of the conversation. I saw that this distinguished man was not moved in the least. I wondered why.

"Professor", he said suddenly, "would it not be better to speak plainly?"

I learned later that the Colonel had obtained a detailed account of our affairs from an inquiry made without my knowledge or that of the President. "Very plainly", he now insisted.

I hedged. I did not wish to implicate others. The Colonel, a fundamentally good person, understood that I was suffering and that I was tired. Knowing that the means of transportation were scarce, he placed a car at my disposal to take me home. He said that he would meet me again. I tried to look pleased, but in my heart I said: If only they would leave me in peace! I felt wholly exhausted.

Around this time I received a visit from Mrs. Laura D. She lived with her family in a house next to ours. We were only slightly acquainted. The reason for her present visit went back some months into the past.

On one of the first days after the invasion of Rome, Miriam said to me in the evening, "This morning I was walking near our house with Giorgio Fiorentino, in search of Hebrews, to warn them to take flight. Mr. D. was smoking a cigarette at the door of his house. I went up to him with Giorgio and said, 'You here? Haven't you heard that my father wants all Hebrews to take flight? I beg you, do take your family and go!' He said, 'Nonsense!' Then he added that a beautiful blonde girl like me ought not to be so panicky. I repeated my advice and left him. It was dangerous to linger, listening to compliments."

What followed? Mr. D. must have thought about it, and without giving the true explanation to his wife, he moved, with his eldest son, to the house of another Jew, a friend of his. But they were deported. Mrs. Laura D. held me responsible, and to avenge the death of her husband and son started an active whispering campaign against me. She became therefore a treasured ally of certain others.

What was the purpose of her present visit? To say that only now had she learned of my daughter's warning and that Giorgio Fiorentino had been witness to it. She expressed her amazement that her husband had not mentioned it to her. Finally she begged pardon. Better late than never, I thought in my heart, and to the lady I said, "Do not worry. These are things that happen in such times."

In a few days, I had my second meeting with Colonel Poletti. The Roman people had taken him to their heart. They would sing, alluding to his radio talks, "Caro Poletti, fewer words and more spaghetti!" And he, smiling, would nod as if to say, "Have more patience, and Poletti will procure you spaghetti."

At this interview, there were three: Colonel Poletti, Captain Newfield, and a Major whose name I do not recall. I found the conversation less fatiguing. The questions were courteous and precise. From time to time, the Colonel would make some rapid comment to the other two in English, which I could not understand, but their facial expressions were sympathetic.

The meeting lasted a long time, almost an hour and a half, but it did not weary me. At the end, Colonel Poletti's companions had nothing to say. "I regret", I said, "the great number of victims. Circumstances were favorable for a work of rescue on a large scale. The Holy Father was filled with active pity. The shortsightedness of some men was a weakness rather than a fault."

The last moment before we parted was solemn. Colonel Poletti stood, and with him the other two. Naturally, I stood also. We remained standing like this, and then the Colonel said, "I feel it my duty to thank you for all you have done. You have done everything within the limits of possibility, giving proof of honesty, foresight, and courage, together with deep wisdom. I thank you and salute you with the hope of seeing you again."

"Strike the iron while it is hot" is a proverb. I had hopes that the letter of Colonel Poletti dated June 30, 1944, and reproduced above would be understood by the President at its real value. It was a good thought. Time heals many things and opens the way to comprehension and better understanding. However, it was not to be. What was the consequence? The decree of July 7, 1944, which follows was the consequence.

Headquarters
Allied Military Government
Rome Region   July 7, 1944
APO 394

                    Administrative Orders
                    Number 135

Considering that the Council of the Roman Jewish Community was elected during the Fascist Regime and during the racial persecution period, and therefore cannot be considered as the expression of the will of the Jews of Rome, and considering the painful events that took place against the Jewish Community during the German domination and the heavy moral and material damage caused to the same Community, and considering the necessity of renewing and rebuilding the life of the Jewish Community of Rome, I, Charles Poletti, Colonel Regional Commissioner of Rome, by virtue of power invested in me,

ORDER

The dissolution of the Council of the Jewish Community of Rome now in office and entrust the temporary administration of the Jewish Community to the Avv. Silvio Ottolenghi with the task of proceeding, at a time to be decided upon, with the new election.

                    Charles Poletti
                    Colonel
                    Regional Commissioner

And thus the Community, split and bleeding in body and disordered in soul, came to find itself under a commissarial regime because certain elements would not disarm. These elements would not allow a breathing spell, nor a brief period of temporary adjustment. They wished that their goal should be reached without losing the force of the discontent and regret aroused by so much zeal. In conformity with the order of Colonel Poletti, I continued to act as Chief Rabbi.

Meanwhile the Ministry of the Interior sent me, by the hands of the Commissioner on September 21, a decree approving my nomination as Head Rabbi and returning to me my Italian citizenship, the racial law being now extinct. The approbation could not have been obtained before because of the fact that I had been declared "apolide", i.e., expelled or exiled, contrary to all justice.

A certain ambiguity of attitude was reflected in the style of the letter in which the approval of my nomination was made known to me:

Rome, 26 September 1944

Excellency Professor Israel Zolli
Head Rabbi, Rome

I am glad to transmit to you the exact copy of the Ministerial Decree of this 21st September relative to the approbation of your nomination as Head Rabbi of this Community.

I am pleased by this definitive provision and I offer my regards.

The Extraordinary Commissioner,
Avv. Silvio Ottolenghi

One day, many years before, while we were talking at mealtime of the political ambitions of so many people, one of my daughters—I don't remember which—had put this question to me: "Father, what would you do if they nominated you Minister of Public Education?"

"See here", I answered, "a university teacher does not run any risk of being nominated to such a high office. It is not likely that they will think of me, but if it should happen, I would accept and take on the office. I would then call the Secretary to dictate to him my letter of resignation, and would stay on, waiting to pass the office to my successor."

"But then why accept?" she asked.

"You do not know your father's love for you! It would make you daughters of an 'Excellency'!" I answered.

Having received the Decree of Approbation from the Ministry, I began to meditate on the idea of resigning. Presently I did so.

Following this resignation I received on January 26 from the new "President" of the Union of the Communities, the letter I here transcribe, omitting the part that concerns the salary and the pension.

Rome 26 January 1945
Lungotevere Sanzio N. 9

Excellency, Professor Israel Zolli
Rome

I am honored to inform you, that in my quality of Government Commissioner of the Union of the Israelite Italian Communities, it is granted to me to call you to direct the Israelite Italian Rabbinical College, which by order of the same date I have reconstituted within the same Community of the Union.

I have left to you the organization of courses and studies, the formation of a Seminary for preparing teachers of religion and Hebrew language for boys and girls.

Your nomination and your taking possession is on stable terms under the following conditions: ..... The center of your office is at the Union of the Israelite Italian Communities, Lungotevere Sanzio 9.

Government Commissioner
Joseph Nathan

Another letter came from the General Headquarters of the Military Allied Government:

Esteemed Professor Zolli   February 1, 1945
Via S. Bartolomeo dei Vaccinari
Rome

Dear Professor Zolli,

In the absence of Colonel Poletti, and in his name, I wish to express the displeasure I felt at the news that on account of reasons of health, you have asked to be released from the charge you have so well fulfilled for many years.

I beg you to accept our best thanks for the collaboration you have given us in this period, which has permitted us to solve many delicate problems concerning your Community.

I wish you in your new and important charges as Director of the Rabbinical College and of your Seminary, all the satisfaction that your honesty, your scientific work deserves and that you may contribute to the reconstruction moral and spiritual of the Italian Israelite Communities.

Maurice Newfield
Captain Q.M.C.
P.A. to R.C.

This courteous letter reached me after I had resigned from my post as Chief Rabbi; I refused to accept the appointment as Director of the Rabbinical College. I was finally free. An interior event that preceded this resignation, I shall now describe, feeling it my duty to open my heart concerning a matter of importance.

16. The Triumph of the Rising Sun

In 1945 light broke forth in my soul. It was the high summer of my spiritual life: after my sorrow a great abundance of fruit issued from the eternally flowering wood of Christ's Cross. He said, "Follow Me." It was the call of God. I followed, receiving baptism in the Roman Catholic Church on February 13, 1945. I had the great joy of being joined in this act by my wife, who received the sacrament with me.

Conversions always come as a more or less agreeable surprise for everyone. Inevitably there is discussion of the causes that have brought the conversion about; and the question is one that is very difficult to resolve. And from the point of view of the convert himself? There too, much will remain obscure. I have never paid any attention to the literature on this subject. I think that it is very hard to create a typology—that is to say, to divide the various conversions and classify them under one type or another. This is a work that one can do sitting at a desk, abandoning living reality: and the product of the undertaking will be only theory, abstracted from reality.

I don't think that the first movements, the growing and maturing processes of conversion, are clearly perceived phenomena even for the convert himself—the man who has *lived* them. By this I do not mean to suggest that this development has taken place in the subconscious, as it is the fashion of today to suppose. I prefer to leave the subconscious out of the present discussion.

If I were to use a simile to express what I have to say

about conversion, I should employ Jesus' own words about the grain of mustard. The seed, embedded in the earth, grows in a hidden manner, and no one heeds its growing. After a time, it manifests itself as the fresh shoot pierces the topsoil; yet it occasions no surprise—only in retrospect has one a confused remembrance of this first appearance. And so in the mind: one does not think about this new development as something to be dealt with, perhaps eliminated. So many stimuli pass through the mind—thoughts and fragments of thoughts, affections: they are born secretly and they die away unheeded. Thus the development of this grain of mustard seed gives rise to no alarm; it is something new in us, and yet it is in no way strange or disturbing, because it is something that, in a very deep sense, belongs to us.

To tell the truth, I could not say that I was quickly aware of the first manifestation in myself of love for the Gospel and for the person of Christ, nor did I welcome it with great tenderness or emotion. No, I received it with the same sentiment with which one receives a member of one's family or a person one loves as a close relation.

The green shoot grows; it becomes stronger and more vivid in color. And this is inevitable. It does not astonish us, because it is part of the whole natural process of development. What is it? In reality it is a new area of knowledge. I mean knowledge and not experience. One's interest in it has nothing in common with the interest one feels in the events of the scientific laboratory, nor even in introspection of the psychological order. I venture to say that, although I took my academic degree in psychology and am deeply interested in psychological problems, I remained quite detached from what was happening within myself, from the point of view of analysis. The event taking place in the depths of my soul

was for me like the arrival of a loved guest. Nothing occurred to give rise to conflict in my conscience. I only began to hear the voice of Christ speaking louder and more
clearly in the Gospels. In my soul, God did not reveal Himself through tempest or fire, but in a gentle murmur. This
may be explained by my character: I am not of a dramatic
temper. Everything in me develops slowly. So in regard to
scientific research and likewise in the sphere of the emotions.

Only now do I understand that Providence has given me a
tendency toward mysticism; but, to speak truthfully, I knew
nothing about this myself. When, some ten years ago, readers of my articles began to notice it, I thought they erred in
judgment. But their number increased, and they were persons wholly unacquainted with one another, living even on
different continents. Then I began to think about a man my
mother used to tell me about when I was a boy. One day
he came home at noon, said good night to everybody, and
went to bed. His wife, much concerned, asked him if he
were ill, and the good man answered: "I am quite well. But
this morning everybody told me that I was drunk. I am not
drunk—you know that I do not even take wine, that I am an
abstainer—but I love peace, and in order not to contradict
them I am going to bed." I felt the same way; I became a
mystic even to myself.

In the years that followed, when the seed of the Christian life that the invisible hand of God had cast into my soul
began to grow with greater vigor, I still did not observe any
conflict between this development and my part as a member of the Jewish religious community. In biblical literature
and in the very abundant rabbinical writings, there is such
a wealth of ideas that one can find much common ground

between Hebraism and Christianity. The lives and ideals of the Christian saints were for me reminiscent of the Hassidic literature (of the Pietists), which I had known since my childhood and loved dearly. The legalistic passages of the Talmud interested me as mental gymnastics, but how much more beautiful and more touching was the Zohar, the cabalistic Bible! I had it in my private library in a three-volume edition—practically pocket books. The Aramaic language of the book seemed easy to me—and then, the language was only the envelope; what was inside was so rich and so stimulating. The interpretations of the Song of Songs that may be found here and there in the Zohar seemed to me far more lovely than those offered by the Aramaic version (the Targum) or even by the Midrash (the rabbinical interpretation).

God began to be more human for me—if I may use such an expression. He was no longer the God of thunder, the God who reveals Himself through the tempest; whose Law is developed and enunciated in so many laws, precepts, and commandments. No, I began to be conscious of a God whom I loved, One who wants to be loved and who Himself loves. I said to myself: From the beginning of the world, men have killed themselves and made their fellow men suffer. They destroy their own lives in order to possess a river, a mountain, a pipeline, a market—and even for the sake of religious doctrines. And sometimes a race comes to regard itself as more gifted and more powerful than all others and sees in this a sign of election, finding in it a new reason to kill.

I began to feel more and more keenly the desire to find someone who would speak to me of the God of Love, the God who loves all without distinction and desires that the bonds uniting men should be those of love. Was this utopia?

That might be, but I told myself: A novelist dreamed of the submarine long before it was ever invented; an artist likewise conceived the airplane. And I began to realize that I had a concrete desire for something like that utopia: I dared to say, the utopia itself.

And I inquired of myself: Surely the realization of my dream of Jesus is not to be merely at the "end of the days", in the prophets' language? Is the sea of love entered only at the end of life? Has not God created us for love? And shall we ascend to God, if we have not loved everyone and everything? This is the path I was treading as I approached the promised land of Christianity.

And still I was conscious of no conflict with Hebraism. God's pilgrims walk on solitary paths. I never spoke about this state of my soul, this growing love, to anybody. The man who loves may feel his love as a burden; but it is a sweet burden which he carries out of inner necessity. "*Amor meus pondus meum*", he says, with Saint Augustine. The man who loves, says Saint Thomas Aquinas, tries to become more and more assimilated to the object of his love. And I loved Jesus; I loved Him ever increasingly.

For many years I had been able to unite Hebraism and Christianity—or was this an illusion? is the idea absurd?—because I loved both. What else could I do?

It was the Day of Atonement in the fall of 1944, and I was presiding over the religious service in the temple. (The German Jews like to call this "the long day", but it is not long; it is a day of enormous content if one is able to comprehend it. I remember, when I was a child, seeing my mother and father weeping during the most touching moments of the Atonement Day service. Now tears have gone out of fashion; I myself cannot weep.) The day was nearing its end, and I was all alone in the midst of a great number of persons. I began to feel as though a fog were creeping into my soul; it became denser, and I wholly lost touch with the men and things around me. A candle, almost consumed, burned on its candlestick near me. As the wax liquefied, the small flame flared into a larger one, leaping heavenward. I was fascinated by the sight of it, looked with wondering amazement at the simple spectacle. I said to myself: In this flame there is something of my own being. The tongue of fire flickered and writhed, tortured; and my soul participated, suffered.

In the evening, there was the last service, and I was there with two assistants, one on my right and the other on my left. But I felt so far withdrawn from the ritual that I let others recite the prayers and sing. I was conscious of neither joy nor sorrow; I was devoid of thought and feeling. My heart lay as though dead in my breast. And just then I saw with my mind's eye a meadow sweeping upward, with bright grass but with no flower. In this meadow, I saw Jesus Christ clad in a white mantle, and beyond His head the blue sky. I experienced the greatest interior peace. If I were to give an image of the state of my soul at that moment I should say: a crystal-clear lake amid high mountains. Within my heart, I found the words: "You are here for the last time." I considered them with the greatest serenity of soul and without any particular emotion. The reply of my heart was: So it is, so it shall be, so it must be.

Nearly an hour later my wife, my daughter, and I were at home for supper after the fast. After supper, my wife took some newspapers and went to her room, and so did my daughter. I remained in my study to write letters and read magazines. When I was tired I went to my bedroom. The door of my daughter's room was shut. Suddenly my wife said to me: "Today while you were before the Ark of the Torah, it seemed to me as if the white figure of Jesus put His hands on your head as if He were blessing you." I was amazed but still very calm. I pretended not to have understood. She repeated what she had just said, word for word. At this very moment, we heard the "Little Trumpet"—so we used to call our younger daughter, Miriam, when she called from afar, "Papaaa!"

I went to her room. "What is the matter?" I asked.

"You are talking about Jesus Christ", she replied. "You know, Papa, tonight I have been dreaming that I saw a very tall, white Jesus, but I don't remember what came next."

I wished them both good night and, wholly untroubled, went on thinking about the unusual concurrence of events. Then I went peacefully to sleep.

It was a few days after this that I resigned my post in the Israelite Community and went to a quite unknown priest in order to receive instruction. An interval of some weeks elapsed, until the 13th of February, when I received the sacrament of baptism and was incorporated into the Catholic Church, the Mystical Body of Jesus Christ.

17. The Charity of Pope Pius XII

"Did you become a convert out of gratitude toward the Pope, who did so much for the Jews of Italy during the Nazi persecution?" This question was addressed to me, and still is, by reporters. In many interviews (inaccurate or invented), they describe me as answering in the affirmative. Why? I suppose to please readers by providing them with a precise and pleasing explanation. In reality, my reply has always been in the negative, but this ought not to be interpreted as a lack of gratitude, and in fact in another book of mine[1] I have emphasized the great charity of the Holy Father and my admiration for him and his work.

As from the Cross of Christ, so from the Chair of Peter, proceed spiritual rays that aim at reaching and illuminating and doing good to all without distinction. One might say of the reign of Pius XII that he is inspired by Isaiah's words: Peace is harmony, peace is salvation, to those near, to those afar off. I want to heal them all.

The Catholic Church loves all souls. She suffers with all and for all; she awaits her children on the sacred threshold of Peter with love, and her children are *all men*. Wisdom, in the Proverbs of Solomon, invites all to her table. The Church, through her visible Head, offers her love and truth and freedom to all. "You shall know the truth and the truth shall make you free" (Jn 8:32).

Jesus Christ spoke of Himself as the "door"; and, again,

---

[1] *Antisemitismo* (Rome: A.V.E., 1945), pp. 244 ff.

He said: "Behold, I stand at the door and knock" (Rev 2:20).
The Vicar of Christ wants all men to be within the sphere of
human and divine charity. Only charity makes men free. At
the very hour in which the terrible sacrificial rite of blood
was initiated, the destruction en masse in the name of race,
of nation, of the state, concentrating the three into one factor: "blood"—precisely then, in the midst of so many fa-
natics, the great Pontiff, unique, serene and wise, exclaims:
"But the legitimate and just love toward one's own country must not close the eyes to the universality of Christian
charity, which also considers others and their prosperity in
the pacifying light of love!"

There is no place of sorrow where the spirit of love of
Pius XII has not reached. Volumes could be written on
the multiform works of succour of Pius XII. The Catholic
priesthood throughout the whole world, religious men and
women and the Catholic laity, stand behind the great Pontiff.
Who could ever tell what has been done? The rule of severe
enclosure falls, every thing and all things are at the service
of charity. As the sufferings grow, so grows the light from
the heart of Christ, and from His Vicar; more vigilant and
ready for sacrifice and martyrdom are his sons and daughters
in Christ. Young Levites and white-haired priests, religious
of all orders, in all lands, dedicated Sisters, all in quest of
good works and ready for sacrifice. There are no barriers,
no distinctions. All sufferers are children of God in the eyes
of the Church, children in Christ, for them and with them
all suffer and die. No hero in history has commanded such
an army; none is more militant, more fought against, none
more heroic than that conducted by Pius XII in the name
of Christian charity.

An old priest who could do nothing further gathered
around him in the church the women and children of the

village (the men had been slaughtered outside the village) so that they might die together in the presence of the crucifix. His dead body is thrown upon the altar, where once he celebrated the Holy Sacrifice, and there he lies, himself sacrificed. An army of priests works in cities and small towns to provide bread for the persecuted and passports for the fugitives. Sisters go into unheated canteens to give hospitality to women refugees. Orphans of all nations and religions are gathered together and cared for. No economic sacrifice is considered too great to help the innocent to flee to foreign lands from those who seek their death. A religious, a most learned man, works incessantly to save Jews, and himself dies a martyr. Sisters endure hunger to feed the refugees. Superiors go out in the night to meet strange soldiers who demand victims. They manage, at the risk of their lives, to convey the impression that they have none—they, who have several in their care.

The attic of one of the great churches in the center of Rome is divided into many sections, each bearing the name of the saint in whose honor the altar below is dedicated. The refugees are divided for the distribution of food into groups according to the names of these saints. Must not the soul of the saint rejoice in such a tribute? Schools, administrative offices, churches, convents all have their guests.

Pope Pius XII is followed by all with the fervor of that charity that fears not death. No one asks for anything except to follow in the footsteps of the Master under the guidance of Pius XII.

At the first hour of his pontificate Pius XII said:

Exactly in times like these, he who remains firm in his faith and strong in his heart, knows that Christ the King is never so near as in trial, which is the hour of fidelity. With a heart broken by the suffering of so many of her children, but with the courage and firmness that come from faith in the Lord's promises, the Spouse of Christ [the Church], advances toward the approaching storm. She knows that the truth she announces, the charity she teaches, and its practice will be the unique counsellors and collaborators of men of good will in the reconstruction of a new world, in justice and love, after humanity, weary of running in the way of error, will have tasted the bitter fruit of hatred and of violence.

Many are the books by statisticians, generals, journalists, and many are the memoirs of individuals concerning this great war. The archives hold quantities of material for future historians. But who, outside of God in heaven, has gathered into his heart the sorrows and the groans of all the injured? Like a watchful sentinel before the sacred inheritance of human pain stands the angelic Pastor, Pius XII. He has seen the abyss of misfortune toward which mankind is advancing. He has measured and foretold the greatness of the tragedy. He has made himself the herald of the serene voice of justice and the defender of true peace. He took into his heart the pain of all the sufferers. He bent over the sorrow of all, and today he stands erect before the whole world saying, "The way you chose was not the just way. The true way is that which leads from the Gospel to Jesus. The good way is marked by a simple and clear word: from the Gospel, with Christ, toward the Kingdom of God."

I did not hesitate to give a negative answer to the question whether I was converted in gratitude to Pius XII for his numberless acts of charity. Nevertheless, I do feel the duty of rendering homage and of affirming that the charity of the Gospel was the light that showed the way to my old and weary heart. It is the charity that so often shines in the history of the Church and that radiated fully in the actions of the reigning Pontiff.

18. The Tears of the Saints

"Was it, then, the Jesuits who converted you?"

This is another question often asked by reporters, who sometimes use the process of elimination to infer the reasons for my conversion from my negative answers.

"No, for many years, since Trieste, I sent contributions to the *Biblical Review*, and sometimes, on the occasion of a trip to Rome, I would visit Father Rector, but the conversion didn't result from that!"

"Then what was it?"

I can say this much: a Jesuit did speak to my heart, Saint Ignatius, founder of the Society. And other saints too: Saint Philip Neri, Saint Francis of Assisi, Saint Catherine of Siena, Alphonse Ratisbonne, whose biography has recently been written, with much competence, by P. H. Colson.

In the category of those who have had a kind of sacred zeal and love with regard to Israel, Saint Ignatius is luminous against a background of historic anti-Semitism. To one of the advocates of untainted blood of his day, the saint said: "I would consider it a special grace had I been of Hebrew origin. What a marvelous thing to be united to Christ, our Lord, and to our Lady, the glorious Virgin Mary, with ties of blood!"

Like Saint Ignatius in this respect was his great friend, Saint Philip Neri. He always prayed for the Hebrew people. So intense was his desire to see the Jews united to Christ, that at the mere sight of one of them still outside the fold, he would weep. One of his disciples, Francis Maria de Ferrara, prayed for three years for the conversion of one Israelite. The day came when he was present at the man's baptism in the Basilica of Saint Peter. "He was", as Father John Oesterreicher gracefully says, "the son of his prayer."

At a time when the Hebrews were the property of the Treasury, "servants of the community", Saint Ignatius and Saint Philip, followers of Saint Paul, prayed with tears: "Let Israel be one with Christ."

In the charity with which God fills the hearts of His saints, there can be no division of race or nationality. We are all of God; every nation, every generation, every man of every religion of every time. The saints are co-citizens of the same kingdom and friends among themselves. They know one another because all are neighbors in the city of God.

God, who is the principle of infinite order, is the God of charity, and God's law is law for man. Darkness and evil are the raw material of which light must free itself. Good must supersede evil, must overcome it. This is the art of living—to fight for the triumph of good, which is charity. In this way, our life must be a work of art, an expression of our will and our genius. Life must not be a surrender to an apparent good that lulls us into a false sense of security, but the fruit of the conscious struggle of the will. Man has the task of reconciling himself with his own ego; with his environment; with his exterior awareness of God, who is Truth and Charity; with God in him, calling him, requiring him to be just and charitable. Man must resist and refuse the contrary elements, the discords within and around him. Harmony and disharmony alike start from within and radiate outward. Harmony must be victorious, and it is the same thing as charity.

The Hebrew convert continues to hear in the Law the voice of the Father. In Jesus, God-made-man, he finds every man. In the shining cloud of the Holy Spirit, he catches vibrations of the song in the souls of the saints. The light emanating from the Holy Spirit is reflected in the mind that approaches the Holy Spirit; in splendor of the Spirit, man is clothed with Christ.

What is the effect of man's conversion, in himself? According to tradition, the Supreme Truth declared to Saint Catherine, "Know, my daughter, that I am He who is, and you are she who is not." Thus speaks Jesus to the soul whom He calls to Himself. Conversion means a new and real knowledge of self, and the soul of the convert hears the words heard by Saint Catherine: "See that you never leave the cell of self-knowledge, but in it keep and use the treasure I gave you, the doctrine of truth, founded on the living stone, Christ, sweet Jesus, whose garment is light. With this clothe yourself, most beloved and sweet daughter, in truth."

Tears acquire value when they are not merely expressive of superficial emotion, but arise from the heart—a *motus proprius* of the soul, expressing interior grief or joy. Only such tears have a voice, a voice inaudible to the physical ear, and yet so powerful that it reaches God's throne.

One day the founder of Hebrew Hassidim (Pietism) was seen during the hour of evening prayer outside a synagogue. His disciples were sure that their master would go in, and they were prepared to follow him; yet he did not enter, but passed on. They followed him. As they passed the second and the third houses of prayer, the same thing happened, and the disciples were filled with amazement. They came then to a small house set back from the street. It was the oratory of the Pietists. Here the master, followed by his own, entered to pray. When they came out, the sky was dark, studded with stars. Seeking an explanation of this behavior they did not understand, one of the disciples asked, "Master, why, when one of us was about to enter one of the other houses of prayer, did you say, 'Not here; it is full of prayers.' Is it not proper for a house consecrated to God to be full of prayers?"

"No, indeed", answered the Rabbi Israel quietly, "and I will tell you why!

"When the faithful enter to implore earthly goods, their prayers become like doves wrought of lead and painted to look real. They have wings but do not fly. Do you understand? But where one enters in order to say to God: 'Lord, I love You, I love You very much. I love You so much that I cannot even tell you how much I love You. I only say: I love You, God who is Love! I am like an instrument that must be played upon, and You alone are the music-maker. It is not I who pray; it is not I who call. I only love, and this, my love, is Yours, this Love is You. In love I, who pray, die; and in You I rise again, and in You I live.' See, my son: these prayers are living doves, pure and newly born; they take flight toward heaven, and so the house of prayer is without prayers. And the power that infuses life into these doves is born of the tears of one who knows how to pray well. Do you understand?" And the Rabbi was silent.

Did he say exactly that? *Exactly* that? No. Probably he spoke in words far more beautiful and lofty than mine. But it is ten years since I read of this episode in the life of Rabbi Israel, the founder of Pietism. I only write what I believe he said.

Although I do not mean to propose my manner of prayer to others, nor to detract from the value of prayers for temporal goods, I nevertheless relate here how I have prayed since my conversion. Five years have passed since then, and I remember very few instances when I prayed for favors for

others, and still fewer when I asked anything for myself.
Once when my wife was very ill, I asked Jesus and Mary
for her cure. Before the *Pietà*, I said: "Thou art a Mother,
a Mother all holy, all holy in sorrow and in love. This sick
woman is a mother." I said no more.

Then turning to Jesus Crucified I prayed: "Lord, Thou
knowest all things. Wilt Thou help me?" In my heart, I heard
His answer, Yes, and I went home so rapidly that I arrived a
little out of breath. We were alone in the house, I was busy,
and I forgot even that I had prayed. My wife's fever continued to rise; she was delirious, and I was crushed by sorrow. Suddenly, at midnight, her condition abruptly changed.
The fever was gone; there was no sign of the eruption the
best physicians available had tried in vain to cure. I could
not believe it. I touched her hand and found it cool. She
began to talk. A few minutes before, she had been beating
her fists against the bed and talking almost unintelligibly in
a distressed way. Now she made some observations about
literature: "Do you know, that last book of yours . . .". I listened somewhat distractedly, but her reasoning was perfect,
she spoke clearly. As I listened I felt troubled by something
I had forgotten trying to come back to my mind. At last it
came to me—the "Yes" of Jesus Christ. "I was helped by
Jesus and by our departed friend, Padre Birolo", my wife
says.

Every time I enter the church with the intention of asking
something of the Lord, I forget to do so. I forget all about
myself, and unfortunately about others also, even when I
have promised. I am ashamed, but it is not quite my fault.
I do not remember, and neither do I forget that I am the
Nothing before the Lord, who is *All*. I would scold myself,
but how could I scold Nothing? Perhaps I do not know how
to pray? It may be.

As a child, ignorant and forgetful of myself, I wept for the sins of others. I sometimes saw my father and my mother weep while they prayed. For scores of years I have wished to see someone weep at prayer, and I have not seen it. And I? I also lost what Padre Cordovani very well defined as "the blessedness of tears". I read about the tears of Saint Ignatius, of Saint Philip Neri, of Saint Francis of Assisi, of Saint Catherine of Siena, but I knew not how to weep with them. During the occupation of Rome I wept for Israel, not for myself. After that I wept no more.

At the moment of baptism and afterward, I did not weep. I saw my daughter, Miriam,[1] weep when she recited the Our Father in the act of baptism a few months after our conversion. (I did not exercise any influence on her decision.) I saw her weep and was not able to weep myself.

A few months later, one morning, I found myself alone in a white room at the Gregorian University. I took a piece of paper and a pencil that were on the table and wrote, without stopping, a few pages in which I gave utterance to my grief for the tears I could not shed. Something was weeping within me, but without tears. The pages written that morning are part of the book *Christus*, published shortly af-

---

[1] My elder daughter, Dora, had no passion for study; she preferred to work at home. It was she who, together with her husband, Victor, sheltered me during part of the German occupation of Rome. The younger, Miriam, on the contrary, had a bent for study, but she was obliged to leave school because of racial laws. She suffered very much on this account and also because she was a very good patriot. Privately she studied languages, and Italian and foreign literature. She was deeply interested in the critique of the art of movies; not from the technical but from the artistic point of view. She published many articles on this subject. Six years ago she began to work in a movie firm, and there she met a colleague, who is now her husband, Dr. Enzo de Bernart. She is the happy mother of the infant Maura Brigida, baptized in the convent of Saint Brigitta.

terward in Italian and later on in Spanish. Let me present
my thought now, briefly, in English:

The books of the Sacred Scripture contain much more
than what is written in them. Our soul also has depths unknown to us. On the sacred pages and in our soul, there
are melodies we do not hear. In the spaces of the world,
there are melodies that no one catches because no one listens. How I weep for this beauty that is lost to us! How I
long for songs without words, sweet harmonies that could
be ours and are not! There are echoes of songs that are as
many songs. There are groans that no one hears, tears that
no one sees or wipes away. There are tables at which no one
sits. There are sanctuaries where no one prays. There is a
nostalgia that no one shares. There are symphonies that no
one hears, something resounding within us and smothered
by us—words not written that nevertheless mean so much.
There are words without echo, questions without answers.

Every word of the prophets, every saying of Christ, is
full of celestial harmonies. We do not treasure what is so
near us; perhaps the Lord's words and our souls have much
to say to us, but we are distracted. Often we are near God
and yet far from God. Near the Book and yet far off. From
afar we perceive a Voice, a Divine Message, and we do not
understand it. A Voice is calling us from afar, and we cannot
follow it. A ray of Light invites us and we do not see it.

It may be that the sadness that invades us and pervades our
soul is due to all that we have lost before we ever possessed
it. It is perhaps the regret of the best and highest part of
our life that we have not lived. Perhaps we are now seeking
what has died and has never been lived.

In the silence of solitary nights, there is still a knock at
the door of my soul. It is the Pilgrim whose call I had not

understood. He ought to have been my Guest, Guest of my soul. Perhaps He has gone; I see Him no more.

The day is far spent. The hour of sunset is not far away. It comes. The harvest is miserable; the flowers to decorate the Lord's altar are few.

Will the Lord gather the tears not yet shed, the harmonies suspended in the air, the songs not yet sung? Will the Lord receive my soul's weeping?

I have nothing except what I have lost, except what I shall never have and what I regret. This regret and this weeping are the only thing that I could still, although unworthily, offer to my Lord. It is the better part of myself.

In the soul of each one of us, Christ lives, Christ who is the way to God, the life of God, the truth of God. He lives in us, and we deny Him. When I feel the burden of my life, when I am conscious of the immense nostalgia of tears not wept, of beauties that have perished unnoticed, I weep over Christ crucified by me and in me. My true self is not the ego that crucified Christ in me, but the "I" who weep and long for Him, who call upon Him, who long to be one with Him.

Having reached the end of this book, I confess that I feel like one dying without having lived: for one fails to live a good life when one fails to live Christ fully. We can but trust in God's mercy, in Christ's pity—Christ, whom mankind puts to death because it does not know how to live Him. We can but trust in the intercession of the one whose heart was transfixed by the same sword that pierced her Son.

Appendix

Because the account I have given of myself during the German occupation of Rome was contradicted by the President of the Community, I feel under the necessity of producing documents to substantiate the statements I have made. Of the following documents, A and B represent the charges made against me by the President; C, D, E, F, G, and H represent testimony offered in confirmation of the truth of my statements.

A. *Verbal of the Session of the BOARD, April 2, 1944 (4 P.M.)*
   Israelite Community of Rome
   Session of the "Giunta" (Board) on April 2, 1944
   (4 P.M.)

ORDER OF THE DAY:

1. Request for payment of stipend to Professor Zolli, Head Rabbi. Present are the Councillors: Foa, Avv., Ugo-President; Cagli Comm., Odo; Levi Comm., Davide Dario; Roccas Avv. Goffredo. The function of secretary performed by: Doctor Fortunato Piperno.

The *President* reads a letter of Professor Zolli, dated February 3, in which he asks for the payment of stipends for him not received in the month of October last.

After setting forth the reasons for which the payment had been suspended, the Board took the following resolution:

Whereas Professor Zolli, on a date previous to the invasion, had made himself undiscoverable, abandoning all religious services and care of souls, the Board, interpreting this attitude, feels that it was the abandonment of a post in the moment in which spiritual assistance of co-religionists was most needed,

resolves

in terms of Article 17 of the R.D. 30 October 1930 n. 1731, and subject to ratification of the Council, declares Professor Zolli, Head Rabbi, dismissed.

As for the request made by him for payment of the stipend, it deems that it cannot be accepted on the basis of the same resolution. It disposes, nevertheless, that in case of need, as for any other co-religionist, financial help be granted to him.

Read and approved during session.
Session ended at 5 P.M.
Secretary
signed F. Piperno

President
signed Foa

Confirmed copy
Secretary ff.
signed F. Piperno

B. Letter of the Community dated July 4, 1944
  Prot. 34 Israelite Community of Rome

Rome, July 4, 1944

Rabbi Professor Israel Zolli
Rome

Illustrious Sir:

I have attentively read the typewritten memorandum dated the 31st of September, that you have sent me. I have the duty nevertheless, for the sake of the facts, to clarify a few affirmations concerning me which are not exact.

1. You have made no request for a conversation with the President of the Union and me, to present a project of yours intended to ward off the danger menacing our co-religionists on the part of the Germans.

2. No note with your signature was given me on September 28th, in which you said that you had assured to the Community a loan of fifteen kilograms of gold. On that day I only had from your daughter a very general promise of eventual help in presence of third parties who will be able to confirm this.

3. Neither by voice nor in writing did you declare to me your readiness to offer yourself as hostage. Furthermore, all your conduct gives the lie to such an affirmation.

   I received from you only one note during the German Occupation. That was in February 1944 and in that note was mentioned exclusively a request for money. So much for the truth.

Best regards,
the President
Ugo Foa.

C. Declaration of Mr. Emilio Prister concerning a prior matter

Rome, Via Nomentana 220 Stairs A., int 9
14 July, 1944

Ecc/mo Comm. Professor Zolli:

I remember very well that in 1933 you did pronounce in the Major Temple of Trieste discourses that condemned the Hebrew persecutions on the part of the Nazis in Germany.

Best Regards,
Emilio Prister

D. Declaration of Doctor Robert Modigliani

Rome, 25 July 1944

Distinguished Professor,

As I had the opportunity to say previously verbally, I remember very well that on a day in the latter part of September of last year, some time after the German occupation of Rome, at the request of your daughter, Miriam, I went to see you at the house of Mr. Anav, where you were staying temporarily. [I remember] how I tried to persuade you to go at once to live with a Catholic family in the hope that you would find there a safer refuge. Although I repeatedly emphasized to you that the opportunity for such a precaution existed, you answered that it was your firm decision to return to your home. You said you were ready to start on the next day, since that day being the Sabbath, you could not have used means of transportation.

I remember that on this occasion, although you were indifferent to your own personal security, you told me that it was your intention to have destroyed, as soon as possible, the lists of the members of the Community; to have the Community itself closed, along with the Temple and the Oratory, suspending all religious functions for the period of the German Occupation.

I remember also that a few days later (at the time of the request for gold), I came to know that only after many Insistences on the part of Miriam had you given up the idea of returning home. Taking refuge with a family that was willing to shelter you, you thus escaped certain capture by the Germans, who had looked for you many times, even forcing the door of your house.

Sincerely,
Robert Modigliani

E. Declaration of the Councillor of the Community
Avv. Ruggero Di Segni, Rome, Lungotevere Altoviti

Rome, 6 July 1944

Esteemed Prof. Comm. I. Zolli
Via St. Bart. dei Vaccinari 19
Roma

Esteemed Professor,

I have received a copy of your note. Since you mentioned me in it, for the exactness of facts, I recall that, after the events of September 8th, I met you only on the 18th of September in an apartment in "Prati" where you were staying temporarily. On that occasion you begged me to inform the Community that for any direct communication, they could telephone to the house of the Avv. Giorgio Fiorentino, which I did. The following day I left Rome on September 19th.

Accept my best regards,
R. Di Segni.[1]

It is true that I refused categorically to reveal the name and address of my host. *This* proved to be undiscoverable indeed, as appeared when the President's personal secretary, Miss Rose Passigli, telephoned to the mother of Fiorentino, the lawyer, to ask the exact address at which I was staying: the street and number. She did not ask to be placed in touch with me.

---

[1] This letter of the Avv. Di Segni, personal friend of the President, in which is written: "*You begged me to inform the Community that for any direct communication, they could telephone to the house of the Avv. Giorgio Fiorentino, which I did*"—this letter contradicts the statement of the President affirming that Professor Zolli on a date previous to the invasion had made himself undiscoverable (see document A).

That I could be reached at any time is evidenced by the episode of the fifteen kilograms of gold. But since in his letter of July 4, 1944, the President declares that: "No note with your signature was given me on September 28th, in which you said that you had assured to the Community a loan of fifteen kilograms of gold" (see document B, sec. 2, above) and "Neither by voice nor in writing did you declare to me your readiness to offer yourself as a hostage" (see document B, sec. 3, above), let us proceed to the autograph of the lawyer Fiorentino.

F. Declaration of the Avv. Dt. Giorgio Fiorentino

At the request of the Most Excellent Head Rabbi of Rome, Professor Israel Zolli, I am able to affirm:

1. That the day preceding the consigning of the gold, Professor Zolli was in possession of a commendatory letter for Comm. Ing. Bernardino Nogana, Head of the Treasury in Vatican City, and was introduced by the Avv. Giuseppe Dieci for abbreviation of formalities.

    I, myself, accompanied Professor Zolli and the advocate Dieci to the Gate of Saint Ann, and I waited at the said entrance till the return of Professor Zolli. He informed me that he obtained, in a manner *private and reserved*, a loan of fifteen kilograms of gold, to be returned without limit of time in equivalent gold or currency, on the simple guarantee of a receipt signed by the Head Rabbi and by the President of the Israelite Community of Rome.

2. That immediately afterward I accompanied Professor Zolli to my dwelling on Via Sforza Pallavicini n. 30, where in my study he wrote a letter to the President of the Israelite Community of Rome, and that he read it to me when finished.

3. *That in said letter Professor Zolli informed the President of the success of his visit to Vatican City, and proposed to him a rough draft of the receipt. That in the same letter the Professor declared that if a demand for hostages on the part of the Germans became unavoidable, he was ready to offer himself among the first and that he was, in all events, at the disposal of the Community for any other task.*

4. That such letter was by me consigned to Miss Miriam Zolli, daughter of the Professor, in order that she should take care of remitting it personally to the President.

   That I, myself, accompanied Miss Zolli to the waiting room of the President, where she was introduced in his presence.

I can affirm this on my word. At your disposal for any further clarification whatsoever.

Giorgio Fiorentino
Via Sforza Pallavicini 30, Rome

G. *Declaration of Miriam Zolli*

I hereby declare that the morning of the day of the delivery of the gold, accompanied by the Avv. Fiorentino, I carried a letter from my father to the President of the Community, the advocate Foa.

I was received at once, consigned the letter personally into the hands of Avv. Foa., many members of the Council being present. I believe that Comm. Vitale Milano was also there; he is the present President of the Community. Because I remember that the safe was open, and in those days he acted as Treasurer. At any rate the room was filled with Councillors and Directors of the Community.

Avv. Foa. took note of the letter in silence, and, at my

request, communicated to those present the generous offer made therein.

I remember that Doctor Renzo Levi, on my return to Rome after the liberation, told me he was glad to have seen me at that time and to hear how much my father had done.

I remember that I also said by word of mouth, that in case hostages were to be given, my father wished to be among the first.

I remember that, despite the word of honor given for secrecy, the news of my father's visit to the Vatican was made public, and when leaving the Temple, I was surrounded by many co-religionists anxious to know the result of the visit. As a witness I remember Gemma Contardi, an usher of the Temple. I begged all in the name of my father to leave their homes, and above all not to congregate around the Temple while the German spies were there. No one in the Community Office had thought as far as that. To any denial of these assertions, I am ready to respond with a solemn oath before the Tribunal.

I remember that on the same morning or the preceding evening, I turned in twelve grains of gold and the sum of five thousand lire from my father as a personal offering to the Community.

In faith of this, I am

Miriam Zolli
Via Ciro Menotti 26

As evidence of the President's attitude toward rescue work in behalf of co-religionists will serve, I believe, the following communication given in writing by Professor Helen Sonnino, the wife of Finzi, and the daughter of the late and lamented Head Rabbi of Genoa. It is a very important document, coming as it does, from a lady most noble in every respect.

H. Declaration of Professor Helen Sonnino-Finzi

Rome, July 2nd, 1944

Most Excellent Professor Zolli Head Rabbi,

As I had occasion to tell you by word of mouth, I confirm that after the consigning of the gold to the German Embassy on the part of the Jews, I had occasion to approach the President of the Community, lawyer and commendatore Ugo Foa. I presented myself and asked whether he thought it opportune that we should leave our homes. He answered me that he saw no necessity and ironically added that he really knew not what dangers could menace me.

Accept my respects,
Elena Sonnino-Finzi

Many other documents that would serve as confirmation of my account of the foregoing events have been scattered, but those I have presented in this Appendix should be sufficient for a just evaluation of the two documents, A and B, both signed by the President.